公式 TOEIC®
Listening & Reading
トレーニング

リーディング編

一般財団法人 国際ビジネスコミュニケーション協会

はじめに

　本書『公式 TOEIC® Listening & Reading トレーニング2　リーディング編』は、TOEIC® Listening & Reading Test のリーディングセクションに対応した教材です。

　　　※ リスニングセクションには、『公式 TOEIC® Listening & Reading トレーニング2　リスニング編』が対応しています。

　本書は、リーディングセクションの学習に力を入れたい方々がより多くの問題を解くことができるよう、**20 セクションに分けて合計 377 問を掲載**しています。問題は全てテスト開発機関 ETS が実際のテストと同じプロセスで制作しています。

　本書を TOEIC® Listening & Reading Test のリーディングセクションの受験準備、そして皆さまの英語学習にお役立ていただけることを願っております。

2023 年 12 月

一般財団法人 国際ビジネスコミュニケーション協会

目　次

※ 各セクションの正解・訳は別冊に掲載しています。

TOEIC® Listening & Reading Test について

TOEIC® Program は、日常生活やグローバルビジネスにおける活きた英語力を測定する世界共通のテストで、現在 4 種類のテストがあります。その 1 つである TOEIC® Listening & Reading Test（以下 TOEIC® L&R）は、「聞く」「読む」の 2 つの英語力を測定するためのテストです。

最大の特長は、テスト結果を合格・不合格ではなく、リスニングセクション 5 点〜 495 点、リーディングセクション 5 点〜 495 点、トータル 10 点〜 990 点のスコアで評価することです。そのスコア基準は常に一定であり、受験者の英語能力に変化がない限りスコアも一定に保たれます。これにより、受験者は正確に現在の英語能力を把握したり、目標とするスコアを設定したりすることができます。

※ 最新の情報については IIBC 公式サイト https://www.iibc-global.org をご参照ください。

TOEIC® L&R の問題形式

●リスニングセクション（約 45 分間・100 問）と、リーディングセクション（75 分間・100 問）から成り、約 2 時間で 200 問に解答します。途中、休憩はありません。
●テストは英文のみで構成されており、英文和訳や和文英訳といった設問はありません。
●マークシート方式の一斉客観テストです。

※ テスト中、問題用紙への書き込みは一切禁じられています。

リスニングセクション（約 45 分間）　　※ 本書ではリスニングセクションの問題は掲載していません。

パート	Name of Each Part	パート名	問題数
1	Photographs	写真描写問題	6
2	Question-Response	応答問題	25
3	Conversations	会話問題	39
4	Talks	説明文問題	30

リーディングセクション（75 分間）

パート	Name of Each Part	パート名	問題数
5	Incomplete Sentences	短文穴埋め問題	30
6	Text Completion	長文穴埋め問題	16
7	・Single passages	1 つの文書	29
	・Multiple passages	複数の文書	25

本書の使い方

本書では、TOEIC® L&R リーディングセクション（Part 5 ～ Part 7）の全 377 問を Section 1 ～ Section 20 の 20 のセクションに分けて学習します。

問題を解く

本冊	問題

8 ～ 9 ページに各パートの Directions（指示文）を掲載しているので、まずこれらの指示文を確認してから、学習を始めましょう。

各セクションには、Part 5 ～ Part 7 の全パートの問題が 18 ～ 20 問【Part 5：7 問／Part 6：4 問／Part 7 [1 文書]：2 ～ 4 問、[複数文書]：5 問】掲載されています。1 つのセクションの目標解答時間は約 15 分です（本番のテストで時間内にリーディング問題全問を解き終えることを想定して算出したもの）。

学習記録

各セクションの最初のページに学習日を記録し、解き終えた後、正解数を記入します。1 回目と 2 回目は全セクションを学習し、2 回目の正解数が 16 問以下のセクションは 3 回目も学習しましょう。

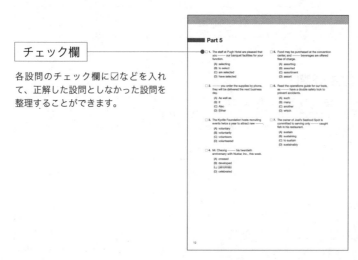

チェック欄

各設問のチェック欄に☑などを入れて、正解した設問としなかった設問を整理することができます。

正解と内容を確認する

別冊　**正解／訳**

各セクションの問題に解答後、別冊で正解を確認しましょう。間違えた設問は本冊のチェック欄に自分なりの方法で印を付けましょう。その後、もう一度英文を読んで和訳を確認し、正解できなかった理由を考えましょう。また音読で復習することもお勧めです。

正解一覧

そのセクションの設問の正解を一覧で掲載しています。

和訳

正解できなかった問題の和訳は特に丁寧に確認しましょう。

1 セクションの進め方の例

※ 1 日に 1 セクションを行えば、20 日間で一通り解き終えることができます。

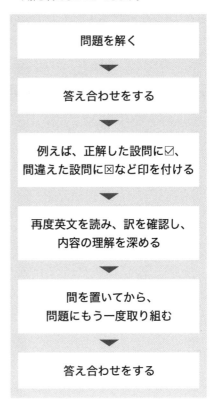

Section 20 まで解き終えたら、もう一度 Section 1 から問題を解いてみましょう。
1 回解答しただけで終わらせず、何度も繰り返して学習することが、英語力向上のために効果的です。

本番の TOEIC® L&R を受験する前に

本書で繰り返し学習を終えた後は、テスト本番の受験に向けて感覚を養うために、『公式 TOEIC® Listening & Reading 問題集』シリーズなどで、リスニングセクションとリーディングセクションの全 200 問を通して解答してみることをお勧めします。タイマーなどを利用して 2 時間計測しながら、休憩を入れずに解答しましょう。実際にマークシートを塗って解答練習を行うことも重要です。その際、時間切れにならずに最後の問題まで解答できるよう、リーディングセクションでは時間配分に注意を払いましょう。

Part 5 〜 7 の問題形式および Directions（指示文）とその訳

本番のテストでは、問題用紙のリーディングセクションの冒頭には、リーディングセクション全体の説明と Part 5 の指示文が、Part 6 〜 7 の冒頭にはそれぞれのパートの指示文が印刷されています。本書の各セクションの学習を始める前にこれらの指示文を読んで、各パートの流れを確認しましょう。リーディングテストのため、音声はありません。

Part 5　短文穴埋め問題

問題数と内容　30 問（Q101 〜 130）。短い英文中に空所が 1 カ所あります。空所を埋めるのに最もふさわしいものを、4 つの選択肢から選びます。

READING TEST

In the Reading test, you will read a variety of texts and answer several different types of reading comprehension questions. The entire Reading test will last 75 minutes. There are three parts, and directions are given for each part. You are encouraged to answer as many questions as possible within the time allowed.

You must mark your answers on the separate answer sheet. Do not write your answers in your test book.

PART 5

Directions: A word or phrase is missing in each of the sentences below. Four answer choices are given below each sentence. Select the best answer to complete the sentence. Then mark the letter (A), (B), (C), or (D) on your answer sheet.

リーディングテスト

リーディングテストでは、さまざまな文章を読んで、読解力を測る何種類かの問題に答えます。リーディングテストは全体で 75 分間です。3 つのパートがあり、各パートにおいて指示が与えられます。制限時間内に、できるだけ多くの設問に答えてください。

答えは、別紙の解答用紙にマークしてください。問題用紙に答えを書き込んではいけません。

パート 5

指示：以下の各文において語や句が抜けています。各文の下には選択肢が 4 つ与えられています。文を完成させるのに最も適切な答えを選びます。そして解答用紙の (A)、(B)、(C)、または (D) にマークしてください。

Part 6　長文穴埋め問題

4文書、16問（Q131～146）。1つの文書に空所（設問）が4カ所あります。文書を読んで、空所を埋めるのに最もふさわしいものを、それぞれ4つの選択肢から選びます。

4カ所の空所のうち、3つは語（句）を選ぶ設問、1つは文を選ぶ設問です。

文書は100語前後の英文で、手紙やEメール、お知らせなどが登場します。

PART 6

Directions: Read the texts that follow. A word, phrase, or sentence is missing in parts of each text. Four answer choices for each question are given below the text. Select the best answer to complete the text. Then mark the letter (A), (B), (C), or (D) on your answer sheet.

パート6

指示：以下の文書を読んでください。各文書の中で語や句、または文が部分的に抜けています。文書の下には各設問の選択肢が4つ与えられています。文書を完成させるのに最も適切な答えを選びます。そして解答用紙の (A)、(B)、(C)、または (D) にマークしてください。

Part 7　［1つの文書／複数の文書］（読解問題）

15セット、54問（Q147～200）。1つまたは複数の文書のセットを読んで、その内容に関する設問に答えます。各設問には4つの選択肢があり、最も適切なものを選びます。

1文書の問題が10セット、複数文書の問題が5セット（2文書問題が2セット、3文書問題が3セット）です。1文書の問題は1セットに2～4つの設問があります（計29問）。複数文書の問題は1セットに5つの設問があります（計25問）。

問題の英文書は、広告、請求書、ウェブページ、記事、Eメール、お知らせ、申し込みフォームなど、さまざまな内容・形式のものが登場します。

PART 7

Directions: In this part you will read a selection of texts, such as magazine and newspaper articles, e-mails, and instant messages. Each text or set of texts is followed by several questions. Select the best answer for each question and mark the letter (A), (B), (C), or (D) on your answer sheet.

パート7

指示：このパートでは、雑誌や新聞の記事、Eメールやインスタントメッセージなどのさまざまな文書を読みます。1つの文書または複数の文書のセットには、それぞれ、幾つかの設問が続いています。各設問について最も適切な答えを選び、解答用紙の (A)、(B)、(C)、または (D) にマークしてください。

Section

1

Section 1 の正解数		
1回目	2回目	3回目
月　　日　　　問／18問	月　　日　　　問／18問	月　　日　　　問／18問

Part 5

☐ **1.** The staff at Pugh Hotel are pleased that you ------- our banquet facilities for your function.

(A) selecting
(B) to select
(C) are selected
(D) have selected

☐ **2.** ------- you order the supplies by phone, they will be delivered the next business day.

(A) As well as
(B) If
(C) Also
(D) Either

☐ **3.** The Kyville Foundation hosts recruiting events twice a year to attract new -------.

(A) voluntary
(B) voluntarily
(C) volunteers
(D) volunteered

☐ **4.** Mr. Cheong ------- his twentieth anniversary with Nustar, Inc., this week.

(A) crossed
(B) developed
(C) performed
(D) celebrated

☐ **5.** Food may be purchased at the convention center, and ------- beverages are offered free of charge.

(A) assorting
(B) assorted
(C) assortment
(D) assort

☐ **6.** Read the operations guide for our tools, as ------- have a double safety lock to prevent accidents.

(A) such
(B) many
(C) another
(D) which

☐ **7.** The owner of Joel's Seafood Spot is committed to serving only ------- caught fish in his restaurant.

(A) sustain
(B) sustaining
(C) to sustain
(D) sustainably

Part 6

Questions 8-11 refer to the following advertisement.

Williamsen Computer Solutions

Is your computer running more ------- than usual? Do you need help installing applications or
8.

upgrading your operating system? ------- . If you require assistance with any number of common
9.

maintenance issues, bring your computer to Williamsen Computer Solutions. Our team of trained

experts will perform a complimentary check of its functionality and ------- the best course of action.
10.

------- us a call today at 555-0165.
11.

☐ **8.** (A) slow
    (B) slowly
    (C) slows
    (D) slowing

☐ **10.** (A) demand
    (B) request
    (C) retain
    (D) recommend

☐ **9.** (A) Are you planning a vacation?
    (B) Do you want a bigger movie selection?
    (C) Would you like to clean your hard drive?
    (D) Have you received a discount coupon?

☐ **11.** (A) Give
    (B) You gave
    (C) To give
    (D) You should have given

GO ON TO THE NEXT PAGE ⟶

Part 7

Questions 12-13 refer to the following instructions.

Congratulations on choosing the best supplies for your office. Inside the box you will find the parts for item #434837, the three-tier desk organizer. This can be installed to hang on your wall, or it can sit on your desk.

To assemble it, you will need:
• A flat-head screwdriver
• Six screws (included)

First, screw the crossbars into the sides of the holder. Do not overtighten the screws. Next, slide the trays into each of the three levels of the organizer.

☐ **12.** Where would the instructions most likely
be found?

(A) On a Web site
(B) Inside a product package
(C) On an office wall
(D) Inside a toolbox

☐ **13.** What is NOT indicated about item
#434837?

(A) It can be put together in two steps.
(B) It includes trays.
(C) It comes with screws.
(D) It requires multiple people for
assembly.

GO ON TO THE NEXT PAGE ———→

Questions 14-18 refer to the following form and e-mail.

Walk Christchurch: A walking tour offered by Walk the World Tours

Thank you for having joined us on a Walk the World tour of the city of Christchurch. Please take a few moments to let us know about your tour so we can continue to offer the best possible experience.

Your name: *Ruben Veiga* **Your e-mail:** *veigar@sucorreio.com.pt* **Tour date:** *10 June*

1. What did you enjoy about the tour?
The views were lovely, and the hotel where we stopped for a delicious lunch was convenient to several shops.

2. What strengths and weaknesses did your tour guide have?
Our tour guide, Janine, was knowledgeable about some topics, but not about architecture. She was friendly, though, and did well in telling us how we should dress for the tour and how long it would take.

3. Did the tour meet your expectations?
Somewhat. The length and difficulty of the walk was what I expected. However, I suggest all walkers be advised to bring water.

4. What else would you like us to know?
The pretour breakfast at 8:30 AM started too late. We felt too rushed to eat before the tour began at 9:00 AM.

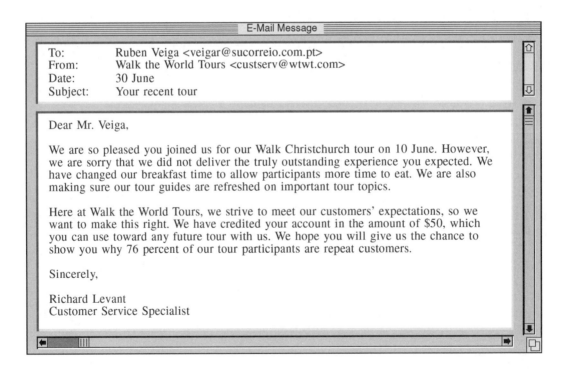

E-Mail Message

To: Ruben Veiga <veigar@sucorreio.com.pt>
From: Walk the World Tours <custserv@wtwt.com>
Date: 30 June
Subject: Your recent tour

Dear Mr. Veiga,

We are so pleased you joined us for our Walk Christchurch tour on 10 June. However, we are sorry that we did not deliver the truly outstanding experience you expected. We have changed our breakfast time to allow participants more time to eat. We are also making sure our tour guides are refreshed on important tour topics.

Here at Walk the World Tours, we strive to meet our customers' expectations, so we want to make this right. We have credited your account in the amount of $50, which you can use toward any future tour with us. We hope you will give us the chance to show you why 76 percent of our tour participants are repeat customers.

Sincerely,

Richard Levant
Customer Service Specialist

☐ **14.** What is the purpose of the form?

    (A) To advise customers about what to bring on a tour

    (B) To seek suggestions for new tour locations

    (C) To obtain feedback on a tour

    (D) To register for an upcoming tour

☐ **15.** What does Mr. Veiga say about Janine?

    (A) She was late leaving for the walk.

    (B) She offered helpful advice before the tour.

    (C) She did not distribute brochures.

    (D) She was knowledgeable about building styles.

☐ **16.** What does Mr. Veiga suggest changing?

    (A) The stops made along the route

    (B) The time breakfast is served

    (C) The hotel selected

    (D) The food offered

☐ **17.** What will most likely happen to Janine?

    (A) She will be moved to a different tour.

    (B) She will start working at a hotel.

    (C) She will receive a discount on breakfast.

    (D) She will be retrained in tour content.

☐ **18.** What is indicated in the e-mail about Walk the World Tours?

    (A) It has many repeat customers.

    (B) It recently added new destinations.

    (C) It has been in business for two years.

    (D) It has reduced the distance of the Christchurch walk.

Section

2

Section 2 の正解数		
1回目	2回目	3回目
月　　日　　　問／18問	月　　日　　　問／18問	月　　日　　　問／18問

Part 5

1. Promotional materials ------- Star Business Academy's courses will be on display at the open house on Sunday.

(A) about
(B) among
(C) into
(D) over

2. Savarini Construction has been the ------- housebuilder in the region for the past decade.

(A) leadership
(B) led
(C) leader
(D) leading

3. Mr. Amal Alsomali has been tasked with ------- mobile technologies at Zoreh Ltd.

(A) oversee
(B) overseen
(C) overseeing
(D) will oversee

4. At Saiko Hinshitsu Insurance, transparency and open communication are high -------.

(A) consequences
(B) priorities
(C) stories
(D) honors

5. The ------- merger of Optera Chemical and Clough Pharmaceuticals is one of many items on the meeting agenda.

(A) occasional
(B) accurate
(C) identical
(D) upcoming

6. The author would like to express her ------- to the editors for their assistance with her novel.

(A) appreciation
(B) appreciate
(C) appreciative
(D) appreciatively

7. Because of ------- weather conditions, the nature walk will be rescheduled.

(A) routine
(B) severe
(C) absolute
(D) concerned

Part 6

Questions 8-11 refer to the following notice.

The Oaktown Classic Cinema (OCC) ------- movie tickets at half price on weekends during the
8.
summer months. The films shown on these summer weekends will mostly include the standard
classic movies that we are known for. We will also, however, offer one ------- film per day, usually
9.
in the evening. ------- . The OCC offers three options, including one for unlimited movies.
10.

The cinema will publish its list of summer movies ------- the end of May.
11.

☐ **8.**　(A) will sell
　　　　(B) sold
　　　　(C) had sold
　　　　(D) sell

☐ **9.**　(A) absent
　　　　(B) mixed
　　　　(C) current
　　　　(D) preliminary

☐ **10.**　(A) The OCC has been in business for
　　　　　　over three decades.
　　　　(B) Besides tickets for individual shows,
　　　　　　monthly passes are also available.
　　　　(C) No outside food or drinks are
　　　　　　permitted, as the theater has a
　　　　　　concessions area.
　　　　(D) Last year, the OCC was closed for
　　　　　　two weeks for renovations.

☐ **11.**　(A) by
　　　　(B) on
　　　　(C) inside
　　　　(D) beside

GO ON TO THE NEXT PAGE ⟶

Part 7

Questions 12-13 refer to the following text-message chain.

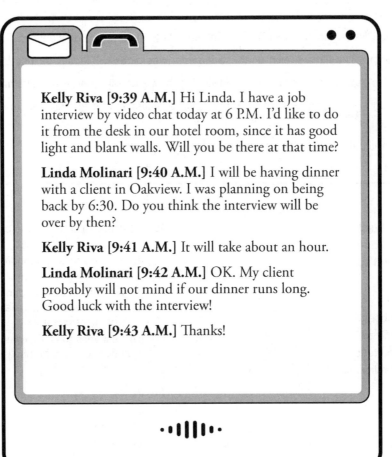

Kelly Riva [9:39 A.M.] Hi Linda. I have a job interview by video chat today at 6 P.M. I'd like to do it from the desk in our hotel room, since it has good light and blank walls. Will you be there at that time?

Linda Molinari [9:40 A.M.] I will be having dinner with a client in Oakview. I was planning on being back by 6:30. Do you think the interview will be over by then?

Kelly Riva [9:41 A.M.] It will take about an hour.

Linda Molinari [9:42 A.M.] OK. My client probably will not mind if our dinner runs long. Good luck with the interview!

Kelly Riva [9:43 A.M.] Thanks!

☐ **12.** What is most likely true about
Ms. Molinari and Ms. Riva?

(A) They are sharing a hotel room.

(B) They work as newspaper reporters.

(C) They live in Oakview.

(D) They are both looking for jobs.

☐ **13.** At 9:41 A.M., what does Ms. Riva imply
when she writes, "It will take about an
hour"?

(A) She would like to join Ms. Molinari
for dinner.

(B) She wants Ms. Molinari to return later
than planned.

(C) She hopes that Ms. Molinari will be
ready for an interview.

(D) She regrets that Ms. Molinari will be
unable to join a video chat.

GO ON TO THE NEXT PAGE ⟶

Executive Summaries for Nonprofits
By Olga Sokolinsky

It is common for nonprofit organizations to apply for funds in order to sustain their operations. Such organizations need to write strong executive summaries to secure the grant money offered by a variety of sponsors, among them foundations, corporations, and government agencies.

The executive summary is an overview that helps the grantor (the organization that provides funding) quickly understand the mission of your nonprofit. It is what a potential grantor will mainly read, among other materials in a grant proposal, when considering a request for money, so it must be written clearly and concisely.

First, it describes what your organization does and what its core values are. Next, it often gives a brief history of the organization and its key personnel. It also highlights significant facts, such as how it has grown or changed. A brief financial summary of all funding sources is usually included.

Polk County Tech Alliance
Executive Summary

Our mission: The Polk County Tech Alliance is a nonprofit organization offering welcoming, low-cost computer classes to residents of Polk County to help them improve their lives.

The Tech Alliance was started three years ago by a small group of educators living in Polk County. They noticed a need for supplementary instruction in computer skills for adults in the county. Developing these skills helps build confidence in students and can help them find good jobs. Beginner to advanced computer classes are now held twice weekly. A local school provides classrooms free of charge. Students pay only $35 for a twelve-week term, and scholarships are available for those unable to pay. The Tech Alliance now serves approximately twice as many students as it did in its first year and expects to draw an increasing number of students in the coming year. Our classes are currently taught by three qualified instructors, and we are planning to recruit an additional one soon.

14. For whom is the article intended?

(A) New residents of Polk County

(B) Job seekers

(C) Technology instructors

(D) Nonprofit groups

15. According to the article, what is the goal of an executive summary?

(A) To comply with government regulations

(B) To profile an organization's leaders

(C) To obtain funds

(D) To attract potential employees

16. What is true about Tech Alliance's executive summary?

(A) It is part of a larger proposal.

(B) It is a revised version of an earlier submission.

(C) It was written by Tech Alliance's instructors.

(D) It was submitted long before the deadline.

17. What is indicated about the Tech Alliance?

(A) It pays a rental fee for its facilities.

(B) Its classes are 35 minutes long.

(C) Its enrollment has recently decreased.

(D) It holds two classes per week for each level.

18. In the executive summary, the word "draw" in paragraph 2, line 8, is closest in meaning to

(A) attract

(B) sketch

(C) instruct

(D) promote

Section

3

Part 5

1. Bon-hwa's Knits announced plans ------- this week to move its Highland Springs store to downtown Richmond.

(A) toward
(B) both
(C) passing
(D) earlier

2. Contractors working on municipal projects must ------- with the city's rules concerning fair hiring practices.

(A) suggest
(B) assume
(C) comply
(D) convey

3. Regional farmers have ------- applied the latest technology to this year's crop-growing practices.

(A) success
(B) successes
(C) successful
(D) successfully

4. The *Grovestreet Gazette* always publishes corrections as soon as they are brought to our -------.

(A) benefit
(B) belief
(C) attention
(D) demand

5. Furnikor's legal department is staying in contact with ------- authorities to ensure that the new building meets all regulations.

(A) location
(B) locating
(C) locate
(D) local

6. Samantha's Sandwiches was able to find a new manager ------- two weeks of Mr. Han's retirement.

(A) since
(B) except
(C) during
(D) within

7. Reanta Financial Group provides funding to entrepreneurs who do not have ------- to traditional loans.

(A) access
(B) accessibility
(C) accessible
(D) accessing

Part 6

Questions 8-11 refer to the following article.

Artist Walks to Find Creativity

Artist and digital content manager Stacy Aham attributes her time-management skills and creative success to a simple habit—a daily walk. Ms. Aham ------- it a point to walk every day, at least for
8.
one mile, around her neighborhood.

"It helps me prepare for the day ahead," said Ms. Aham. "About six months ago, I canceled my gym memberships and exercise classes. I basically decided to leave my car on the driveway most of the time, and now I just walk ------- . I'm the healthiest I've ever been. Wandering around
9.
free of purpose also helps me discover artistic ideas," she says. "The natural surroundings inspire me. ------- ."
10.

Ms. Aham ------- feels more confidence in her ideas and is better able to focus on her goals.
11.

□ **8.** (A) made
(B) makes
(C) will make
(D) had made

□ **9.** (A) anything
(B) something
(C) everywhere
(D) elsewhere

□ **10.** (A) I'm always sure to wear a coat.
(B) It probably won't be this way for long.
(C) I expect to return to work next month.
(D) This is especially true in the springtime.

□ **11.** (A) consequently
(B) summarily
(C) adversely
(D) briefly

GO ON TO THE NEXT PAGE ⟶

Part 7

MEMO

To: Viateur Hotel staff
From: Fiona Donlon, General Manager
Date: January 17
Subject: Important information

We will be replacing all light bulbs in our hotel with bulbs that are more energy efficient. Our maintenance staff will start making this switch on Monday. They will begin with the light fixtures in the lobby and hallways, then move on to individual guest rooms. You do not need to change anything about your usual work routine. I just want to make sure you are aware that there will likely be more activity than usual here over the next week or two.

Do what you can to keep the hallways clear. Please stay out of the crew's way so the work can be completed as efficiently as possible. This is just one of several changes we are implementing to reduce energy costs here at Viateur Hotel.

Thank you for your cooperation.

12. What is the purpose of the memo?

(A) To announce a new service for guests

(B) To provide details about a special offer

(C) To describe some upcoming work

(D) To invite staff to an event

13. The word "clear" in paragraph 2, line 1, is closest in meaning to

(A) easy

(B) narrow

(C) empty

(D) bright

14. What does Ms. Donlon mention about changes at the hotel?

(A) They are in response to a new governmental policy.

(B) They are intended to save money.

(C) They will serve to attract more business.

(D) They will result in fewer available rooms.

GO ON TO THE NEXT PAGE ⟶

Questions 15-19 refer to the following article, schedule, and e-mail.

Bookstore to Hold Grand Opening

RIVERTON (May 20)—The Riverton Bookstore will celebrate its grand opening on Saturday, May 26, with a lineup of Manitoban literary and musical guests.

Local writers will read from recent publications and autograph books on display in the Reading Nook, on the store's first floor. Musicians have been invited to entertain at the Cozy Café on the second floor. Complimentary treats will be provided by the bookstore's neighboring businesses, the Eastside Vegetarian Restaurant and the Little Bakery.

The store is a business collaboration between Ralph Washington, a historian who has done extensive research in this region, and Paolo Arellano, a former advertising executive. They are passionate about local history and dedicated to promoting new writers.

Riverton Bookstore
Schedule for May 26

12:15–1:00 P.M.	Folk-rock duo Paul and Dennis perform tunes from their album *Morning Key.*
2:00–2:45 P.M.	Fiction writer Vikram Iyer reads from his best seller *Avalon Holiday.*
3:00–3:45 P.M.	Joni Beck plays soothing jazz and blues on acoustic guitar.
4:00–5:00 P.M.	Poet Richard Carney reads from his award-winning collection *Fool's Mask.*

```
╔══════════════════════════════════════════════════╗
║                    *E-mail*                        ║
╠══════════════════════════════════════════════════╣
```

To:	Vikram Iyer <vikrami22@qmail.com>
From:	Paolo Arellano <parellano@rivertonbookstore.ca>
Date:	May 30
Subject:	Thank you

Hello, Vikram,

Thank you for participating in our opening last weekend. The customers enjoyed your reading and talk immensely. Look for a story about our successful event in the next issue of *The Riverton Times*. My business partner was able to take some nice candid snapshots of you during your reading, and we hope they will accompany the story.

Please plan to make a return appearance when your next book is released in June. You are always welcome at our bookstore!

Paolo Arellano

15. According to the article, what is true about Mr. Arellano?

(A) He wrote a book about Riverton.
(B) He owns several businesses.
(C) He has had more than one career.
(D) He lives in a historic house.

16. Where did Paul and Dennis play on May 26?

(A) At the Reading Nook
(B) At the Cozy Café
(C) At the Eastside Vegetarian Restaurant
(D) At the Little Bakery

17. According to the schedule, when did a jazz musician perform?

(A) At 12:15 P.M.
(B) At 2:00 P.M.
(C) At 3:00 P.M.
(D) At 4:00 P.M.

18. What did Mr. Washington most likely do at the grand opening?

(A) He took pictures of an author.
(B) He read from his best-selling book.
(C) He signed bookstore merchandise.
(D) He met with local historians.

19. What does the e-mail indicate about Mr. Iyer?

(A) He invested money in a bookstore.
(B) He arrived late for an event.
(C) His recent talk will be available online.
(D) His new book will be published soon.

Section

4

Part 5

1. Beijing Air's ------- renovated seating will leave travelers relaxed and refreshed by the end of the flight.

   (A) hardly
   (B) always
   (C) newly
   (D) least

2. ------- interested in helping Ms. Page to plan the staff picnic should contact her directly.

   (A) Whose
   (B) Those
   (C) What
   (D) That

3. Customers prefer Orbando blinds and drapes, thanks to their ------- construction and attractive designs.

   (A) sturdy
   (B) intense
   (C) forceful
   (D) healthy

4. The images must be approved by 5:00 P.M. if the team is ------- the launch goal of April 15.

   (A) to meet
   (B) meet
   (C) met
   (D) being met

5. The surplus in the city's discretionary fund was ------- between the school system and the parks commission.

   (A) divided
   (B) signed
   (C) meant
   (D) placed

6. Flaws in the recordings are ------- detectable but can be heard at a high volume.

   (A) specifically
   (B) barely
   (C) recently
   (D) previously

7. ------- the building renovations are complete, the marketing department will work out of the company's branch office in Edinburgh.

   (A) Likewise
   (B) Due to
   (C) Until
   (D) Otherwise

Part 6

Questions 8-11 refer to the following press release.

SINGAPORE—Goh Tech Global, Singapore's top ------- of accounting and finance software, has
8.
announced the appointment of Grace Ng as its new chief operating officer. The appointment is
part of an ------- restructuring plan. Ms. Ng comes to Goh Tech Global with more than
9.
fifteen years of executive experience in the industry, including as COO at Singapore-based
Ridgeco Industries. "We are glad to have Ms. Ng assume this role at such an important stage of
growth in our company," states Alan Chiang, CEO of Goh Tech Global. "------- . She
10.
------- our position as a technology company." Ms. Ng will start at Goh Tech Global on 15 May.
11.

---

8. (A) provider
(B) opponent
(C) associate
(D) method

9. (A) alarming
(B) ongoing
(C) infrequent
(D) instant

10. (A) She used to be well-known for that.
(B) This had happened before, so many employees were unsurprised.
(C) Her expertise will help us as we move forward.
(D) Similar opportunities will become available.

11. (A) had strengthened
(B) was strengthening
(C) will strengthen
(D) strengthen

GO ON TO THE NEXT PAGE ⟶

Part 7

Questions 12-13 refer to the following postcard.

Postcard

Place
Stamp
Here

20th Annual Lilac Festival

Join us May 1 to May 24 at the Vernonville Lilac Festival. Fresh flowers, food, beverages, gifts, and a children's play area will be available for the whole family. Please note that we have new hours this year. We will be open from 8:00 A.M. to 7:00 P.M. daily, rain or shine.

For busy weekends, we recommend purchasing tickets online ahead of time to avoid the ticket booth lines. Visit our Web site at www.vvlilacfestival.org. For large groups of ten or more, call our office at 616-555-0137 to discuss reduced group-ticket pricing.

12. What is indicated about the festival?

    (A) It takes place every two years.

    (B) It is open only on weekends.

    (C) Its location has moved.

    (D) Its hours have changed.

13. What is suggested about large groups?

    (A) They can obtain a discount.

    (B) They can gain early admission.

    (C) They must register at a Web site.

    (D) They must purchase tickets in advance.

GO ON TO THE NEXT PAGE ⟶

Questions 14-18 refer to the following rules, chart, and review.

Sparrow Root Orchard

Pick-Your-Own Rules

1. Pick only what you intend to purchase. Fruit will be paid for by weight upon leaving the orchard.
2. Pick fruit only in designated areas, and put fruit in the containers provided to you.
3. Children must be accompanied by an adult.
4. Do not climb or shake trees.

Sparrow Root Orchard

Pick-Your-Own Harvest Calendar

	June	July	August	September
Strawberries	●			
Peaches		●	●	
Blueberries	●	●	●	
Apples				●

http://www.localfunactivities_marimount/reviews/sparrow_root_orchard

Review ★★★★☆

Reviewer: Ismael Elmon

My family and I enjoyed our first visit to Sparrow Root Orchard. The apples we picked were so delicious! During the enjoyable tractor ride to the orchard, the tractor driver explained the apple picking rules. Bags for the apples were conveniently placed at the end of each row of trees in the orchard. My kids loved climbing up the ladders to pick fruit from high branches. Unfortunately, we did see another visitor shaking one of the trees to try to get the fruit to fall off, but a staff member intervened. A minor downside is it was difficult to find parking in the small parking lot; if anything, it is proof of the orchard's popularity!

☐ **14.** What do the rules indicate about Sparrow Root Orchard?

(A) It encourages visitors to sample the fruit.
(B) It charges for fruit by weight.
(C) It offers programs for children.
(D) It asks visitors to bring reusable containers.

☐ **15.** What fruit has the longest harvest season at Sparrow Root Orchard?

(A) Strawberries
(B) Peaches
(C) Blueberries
(D) Apples

☐ **16.** What does the review mention about the tractor driver?

(A) He told visitors the rules of the orchard.
(B) He assisted Mr. Elmon with parking.
(C) He offered tips on choosing the best fruit.
(D) He climbed a ladder to help Mr. Elmon.

☐ **17.** What rule did Mr. Elmon see a visitor break?

(A) Rule 1
(B) Rule 2
(C) Rule 3
(D) Rule 4

☐ **18.** When did Mr. Elmon visit the orchard?

(A) In June
(B) In July
(C) In August
(D) In September

Section

5

Section 5 の正解数		
1 回目	2 回目	3 回目
月　　日　　　問／20 問	月　　日　　　問／20 問	月　　日　　　問／20 問

Part 5

1. Ted Drabik has ------- become the top salesperson in the electronics department.
   - (A) quick
   - (B) quickly
   - (C) quicker
   - (D) quickness

2. ------- remodeling a home, remember to budget for unforeseen expenses.
   - (A) Still
   - (B) Neither
   - (C) That
   - (D) When

3. Several factors can ------- the quality of the videos streaming on our Web site.
   - (A) affect
   - (B) to affect
   - (C) be affected
   - (D) affecting

4. Once a shopper enters the store, a greeter should ------- offer assistance.
   - (A) closely
   - (B) highly
   - (C) politely
   - (D) lately

5. Ms. Suh was not available to work yesterday, so Mr. Dodd substituted for -------.
   - (A) her own
   - (B) her
   - (C) she
   - (D) herself

6. Mr. Rodrigues thinks that the article in *Acumba Weekly* will bring welcome ------- to the farm's greenhouse project.
   - (A) publicize
   - (B) publicity
   - (C) publicist
   - (D) publicized

7. The Seahurst Building features electrically controlled window glass that transforms ------- clear to opaque in less than a minute.
   - (A) from
   - (B) against
   - (C) between
   - (D) throughout

Part 6

Questions 8-11 refer to the following notice.

The Barrowhill Village Library will be closed for the month of August. After several decades of

------- the community, we have decided it is time to refurbish our building. There will be two
8.

stages to the ------- . We will begin by installing new windows in the inner lobby. ------- .
9.   10.

Patrons who check out books during the last two weeks of July may keep them ------- the work on
11.

the building is completed. This means that those books will be due back on September 1.

---

8. (A) serving
   (B) served
   (C) to serve
   (D) had served

9. (A) discussion
   (B) contest
   (C) renovation
   (D) research

10. (A) The library also has a multimedia room.
    (B) Rather, we will hire more library staff.
    (C) The library is next to the village museum.
    (D) Then we will repaint the entire library.

11. (A) until
    (B) around
    (C) where
    (D) which

GO ON TO THE NEXT PAGE ⟶

Part 7

Questions 12-15 refer to the following text-message chain.

Liza Cho [1:16 P.M.] Hi all. I wanted to remind you that Emily Doley is starting on Josh's team on Monday. Does she have an appointment with the security office to get her identification badge?

Justin Bezuti [1:20 P.M.] I don't see her name on the list online. It seems she hasn't been scheduled yet.

Liza Cho [1:22 P.M.] Can you make sure that her appointment is first thing in the morning, before her orientation?

Justin Bezuti [1:24 P.M.] Definitely. I'll call the security office now.

Josh Hyuk [1:27 P.M.] She'll attend an orientation at 10, and around 11 a technician is scheduled to help set up her workstation. After lunch, I'd like her to meet with each department head. That should take all afternoon.

Chun-Wei Kang [1:28 P.M.] I also need to speak with her about her paychecks. Ideally, that should happen on the first day, but it can be pushed back to Tuesday morning if needed.

Liza Cho [1:29 P.M.] Thanks for accommodating. She still has some personnel paperwork to fill out, and I want to review the new-employee handbook with her in case she has any questions about employee benefits. I can do that around 11:45, just before lunchtime.

Justin Bezuti [1:29 P.M.] OK. I'll finalize her agenda and circulate it later today for confirmation.

12. What will Ms. Doley most likely do first on Monday?

(A) Attend an orientation session
(B) Learn about employee benefits
(C) Visit the security office
(D) Set up her workstation

13. When will Ms. Doley most likely begin meeting department heads?

(A) At 10 A.M.
(B) At 11 A.M.
(C) At noon
(D) At 1 P.M.

14. At 1:29 P.M., why does Ms. Cho write, "Thanks for accommodating"?

(A) Ms. Kang can change a meeting time.
(B) Mr. Bezuti will contact Ms. Doley.
(C) Mr. Hyuk has redrafted a schedule.
(D) Ms. Doley's paperwork has been processed.

15. Who will distribute Ms. Doley's Monday agenda?

(A) Ms. Cho
(B) Mr. Bezuti
(C) Mr. Hyuk
(D) Ms. Kang

GO ON TO THE NEXT PAGE ⟶

Questions 16-20 refer to the following e-mail and invoice.

```
╔══════════════════════ *E-mail* ══════════════════════╗
```

From:	Amrita Patnaik <a.patnaik@godavaririverinn.in>
To:	Raj Doshi <raj.doshi@delhimail.in>
Sent:	Tuesday, 14 July, 6:23 A.M.
Subject:	Room reservations

Dear Mr. Doshi,

Thank you for booking another stay at the Godavari River Inn. This message is to confirm your room reservation for 4 and 5 August. I have added the reservation to our online calendar and will be calling you later today for your credit card number to finalise the reservation. Please rest assured, no payment will be processed until the end of your stay.

Per your request, we have also reserved Conference Room B. It will be set up with seating for twenty guests, audiovisual equipment, and tea service. Please let us know if you have any other requirements for your meeting. I will be available to help work out any technical issues you may encounter.

We look forward to seeing you again.

Sincerely,

Amrita Patnaik, Innkeeper

Godavari River Inn • Trimbake Road, Nashik • Maharashtra 422007

Guest Information	Raj Doshi	**Room Number**	105
	T 298, Main Market	**Room Rate**	₹ 500 / night
	Delhi	**Arrival**	3 August
	110055	**Departure**	7 August

Date	Description	Rate	Balance
3–7 August	Room Charge	₹ 500	₹ 2,000
4 August	Room Service	₹ 150	₹ 150
5 August	Conference Room B	₹ 600	₹ 600
5 August	Tea Service	₹ 200	₹ 200
5 August	Room Service	₹ 150	₹ 150
6 August	Godavari River Inn Bistro (continental breakfast)	₹ 200	₹ 200
		Total:	₹ 3,300

16. What did Ms. Patnaik most likely do on July 14?

(A) She called Mr. Doshi.
(B) She charged Mr. Doshi's credit card.
(C) She prepared a tea service.
(D) She purchased audiovisual equipment.

17. In the e-mail, the phrase "work out" in paragraph 2, line 3, is closest in meaning to

(A) exercise
(B) complete
(C) decide
(D) resolve

18. What is suggested about Mr. Doshi's stay at the Godavari River Inn?

(A) It was longer than originally planned.
(B) It was his first visit to the inn.
(C) It was arranged by his assistant.
(D) It was less expensive than he anticipated.

19. When did Mr. Doshi most likely attend a meeting?

(A) On August 3
(B) On August 4
(C) On August 5
(D) On August 6

20. What is indicated about the Godavari River Inn?

(A) Its conference rooms are off-site.
(B) It has its own restaurant.
(C) It is located in Delhi.
(D) It offers discounts to repeat customers.

Section

5

Section

6

Part 5

1. The inspector noted that the library will need a new roof ------- the next five years.

(A) about
(B) beneath
(C) within
(D) above

2. Veloque Ltd. has hired a communications specialist to ------- its social media content.

(A) expect
(B) occupy
(C) manage
(D) pronounce

3. A list of ------- for local entrepreneurs was recently published in *Bergans Business Journal*.

(A) resourcefully
(B) resourceful
(C) resourced
(D) resources

4. At Jespersen Tailors, measurements are taken twice to ensure ------- sizing.

(A) efficient
(B) probable
(C) remarkable
(D) accurate

5. McLane-Winn is a major textile distributor with offices in more than thirty -------.

(A) situations
(B) locations
(C) connections
(D) professions

6. Effective writers often ------- their sentence structure to maintain the reader's interest.

(A) were varied
(B) varying
(C) vary
(D) to be varied

7. Octipro CEO Leora Han presented ------- of the retiring employees with a special gift.

(A) whatever
(B) ours
(C) this
(D) each

Part 6

Questions 8-11 refer to the following invitation.

The San Pedro Society of Photographic Artists invites you to its ------- retreat at Rio Bayas
                                                                       8.
Conference Center from July 21 to July 24. This event is an opportunity for serious

photographers to meet and share ------- work in a peaceful, scenic location each year. This year,
                                  9.
the program will be expanded to include both morning and afternoon sessions. ------- are asked
                                                                              10.
to bring several prints or digital files of work to introduce at each of the sessions. The cost of the

retreat is $800 and includes room, meals, and gratuities. ------- .
                                                          11.

- [ ] **8.** (A) initial
  - (B) monthly
  - (C) early
  - (D) annual

- [ ] **9.** (A) they
  - (B) their
  - (C) them
  - (D) themselves

- [ ] **10.** (A) Participants
  - (B) Organizers
  - (C) Candidates
  - (D) Supervisors

- [ ] **11.** (A) The conference center hosts many exhibitions.
  - (B) Nonmembers are asked to pay an additional $25 program fee.
  - (C) The society accepts photo submission requests via e-mail only.
  - (D) Most of our members prefer to use lightweight digital cameras.

Section 6

GO ON TO THE NEXT PAGE ———→

53

Part 7

Questions 12-13 refer to the following sign.

WESTOVER BUILDING
Directory

Phi Import Services ....Suite 100	Rivera & Pao Law........................Suite 200
Starcrest Insurance, Inc............Suite 145	Cormac Advertising...................Suite 255
Callon Hill Lending ....Suite 180	Burchell Investment Group......Suite 275

Leasing and maintenance by Kellan Holdings, 555-0198

☐ **12.** Where is the sign most likely posted?

   (A) At a hotel reception desk
   (B) At a shopping mall
   (C) In a law office
   (D) In a building lobby

☐ **13.** What service does Kellan Holdings probably provide?

   (A) Employment counseling
   (B) Property management
   (C) Business investing
   (D) Architectural design

GO ON TO THE NEXT PAGE ⟶

Questions 14-18 refer to the following e-mail and proposal.

To:	Rebecca Hogan <rhogan@aldfairmarket.com>
From:	Alex Griffith <agriffith@swynhaminternational.com>
Date:	April 16
Subject:	Aldfair Market proposal
Attachment:	📎 Proposal

Dear Ms. Hogan:

Attached please find Swynham International's proposal for a new heating and air-conditioning unit for Aldfair Market. Based on our telephone discussion of last Tuesday about the size of your operation and your plans to expand, I am recommending a 3-ton, 110,000 BTU unit. This size should be sufficient for your heating and cooling needs for the next four to six years, up until your planned expansion of the store.

The proposal lists the total cost, including the price of the unit with sales tax and shipping costs. We are able to offer you this very favorable pricing based on current shipping costs (as of this month only). To lock in this rate, please indicate your acceptance by phone or e-mail within fourteen days. Note that, if desired, we can also offer installation by our partner in your area, Kermec Company, at an additional low cost.

Please let me know if you have any questions.

Sincerely,

Alex Griffith
Director of Sales, Swynham International Heating and Air-Conditioning

---

Swynham International Heating and Air-Conditioning
14782 East Hartwick Road, Detroit, MI 48205

Proposal date: April 16
Submitted to: Aldfair Market, 561 Bartlett Street, Alpena, MI 49707
Attention: Rebecca Hogan

Recommended unit: 3-ton, 110,000 BTU Gas Heating/Electric Cooling Rooftop
Unit (unit comes with 10-year manufacturer's warranty)
Model number: BVOHTF77592

Price of unit:	$3,700.00
Sales tax (6%):	$222.00
Shipping:	$175.00
Total cost:	$4,097.00

Installation available for $350.00 by local partner.

14. What did Mr. Griffith most likely discuss by phone with Ms. Hogan?

   (A) Swynham International's four-year sales plan

   (B) Aldfair Market's heating and cooling needs

   (C) Ms. Hogan's plan to visit Detroit in May

   (D) Driving directions to Aldfair Market

15. Why is the estimate given in the e-mail valid for only fourteen days?

   (A) Installation cannot be scheduled more than two weeks in advance.

   (B) The sales tax will increase next month.

   (C) A warranty will expire.

   (D) Shipping costs may increase.

16. What does the proposal indicate about the recommended unit?

   (A) It is designed to be installed on a building's roof.

   (B) Its price has been heavily discounted.

   (C) It will take two weeks to be shipped.

   (D) It will be delivered in two separate packages.

17. For how many years is the recommended unit guaranteed by the manufacturer?

   (A) Four

   (B) Six

   (C) Ten

   (D) Fourteen

18. How much would the work by Kermec Company cost?

   (A) $175.00

   (B) $222.00

   (C) $350.00

   (D) $4,097.00

Section 6

Section

7

Section 7 の正解数		
1回目	2回目	3回目
月　　日　　　問／18問	月　　日　　　問／18問	月　　日　　　問／18問

Part 5

1. All grant proposal submissions must ------- a full committee review.
   - (A) examine
   - (B) transfer
   - (C) estimate
   - (D) undergo

2. Anyone ------- to give a presentation at the quarterly meeting should contact Mr. Jamak.
   - (A) had wished
   - (B) wished
   - (C) would wish
   - (D) wishing

3. Mr. Sousa discovered that ------- wiring was the cause of the malfunction.
   - (A) faulty
   - (B) patient
   - (C) sufficient
   - (D) uneasy

4. The audit results produced by the accounting department were on time and -------.
   - (A) precise
   - (B) precision
   - (C) preciseness
   - (D) precisely

5. Ruth Ann Beachell is a talented woodworker ------- pieces are known for their elegant design and simple utility.
   - (A) as
   - (B) how
   - (C) most
   - (D) whose

6. Included in the cost of admission to the Krogh Architectural Museum is an ------- illustrated catalog.
   - (A) attraction
   - (B) attractor
   - (C) attractively
   - (D) attracted

7. Over the past year, Professor Ott has done ------- research on the history of Oaktown.
   - (A) temporary
   - (B) extensive
   - (C) artificial
   - (D) immediate

Part 6

Questions 8-11 refer to the following article.

CRAIGSBORO (July 21)—Gildermere Park will open its gates to the public on Saturday, July 26, after a five-year project to transform the former golf course into a community recreation area. The new park will offer roughly 25 kilometers of walking and biking trails, as well as two small botanical gardens.

------- .
8.

Craigsboro mayor Steven Ramanithy is expected to attend the official opening along with county officials and local residents. ------- , the event could draw more than 400 people. The mayor,
9.
------- has been a vocal proponent of the park's development, notes that the park will enable
10.
more people in the area to enjoy fresh air and physical exercise on a regular basis. Moreover, the park is being heralded by community leaders as a ------- step forward in environmental
11.
conservation efforts locally.

8. (A) Some park users have not been locking their bikes.
(B) One of the gardens will feature flowers native to the region.
(C) Instead, a ten-kilometer stretch of road will be repaved.
(D) These will be handed out to visitors on the day of the opening.

9. (A) By comparison
(B) Previously
(C) In all
(D) For example

10. (A) his
(B) either
(C) who
(D) another

11. (A) significantly
(B) significance
(C) signify
(D) significant

GO ON TO THE NEXT PAGE ———→

Section 7

Part 7

Questions **12-13** refer to the following e-mail.

To:	Research and Development Staff
From:	Laurel Altmann
Date:	July 10
Subject:	Dr. Decker

Dear colleagues,

After fifteen years at Marabay Labs, senior research scientist Rosamond Decker is leaving to move to New Zealand, where she will be joining the engineering faculty at Wareham University. A farewell party for Dr. Decker will be held at Bistro Georgiana on July 24 at 7 P.M. We will be celebrating her accomplishments at Marabay and presenting her with a gift to wish her well as she returns to teaching, one of her passions.

To indicate that you plan to attend, please register at www.marabaylabs.com/events/4591 so that we know how many people to expect. If you would like to make a donation toward the gift, contact Jake Woloch at extension 256.

Kind regards,

Laurel Altmann, Administrative Manager
Research and Development

12. Why did Ms. Altmann send the e-mail?

(A) To invite employees to a celebration

(B) To introduce a newly hired scientist

(C) To announce an award recipient

(D) To inform employees about a staff
     promotion

13. What is suggested about Dr. Decker?

(A) She is originally from New Zealand.

(B) She has made a donation to Marabay
     Labs.

(C) She is training Mr. Woloch.

(D) She has accepted a teaching
     position.

GO ON TO THE NEXT PAGE ⟶

Questions 14-18 refer to the following guidelines and e-mails.

Camhurst Herald
Guidelines for Reader Submissions

As the town newspaper of Camhurst, we welcome guest columns and letters that present the different perspectives of local readers. Please send them to Carl Shen, c_shen@camhurstherald.com. The deadline for submissions is Monday. The weekly issue is mailed to paid subscribers every Friday.

• Guest columns are a maximum of 500 words long and can be on any topic, although we give preference to matters of local concern. The author must provide a profile photo.

• Letters to the editor are limited to 300 words and must address a local matter.

All submitted columns and letters must present reasonable, fact-based arguments and express opinions with civility. We do not publish press releases or petitions.

Although lack of space prevents us from printing all the submissions we receive, you can find them online at www.camhurstherald.com/opinion.

To:	c_shen@camhurstherald.com
From:	mona.herrera@cranmail.net
Date:	April 1
Subject:	Reader submission
Attachment:	Zoning; M.Herrera_Photo

Dear Mr. Shen,

On March 29, the *Camhurst Herald* published an editorial about the new zoning regulations that are currently under consideration by the town council. As a new franchise owner, I've been following this topic closely. I think the writer is mistaken to claim that the regulations will discourage people from opening retail businesses downtown. I'm submitting the attached response, together with the required photograph.

Thank you,

Mona Herrera

To:	mona.herrera@cranmail.net
From:	c_shen@camhurstherald.com
Date:	April 9
Subject:	Re: Reader submission

Dear Ms. Herrera,

Thank you for your voicemail message following up with me about last week's issue. The news about the increase in the property tax pushed everything else aside, including the reader submissions. Yours meets our standards and thus will appear in next week's print issue. Thank you for your patience.

Best regards,

Carl Shen

14. What do the guidelines suggest about the *Camhurst Herald*?

(A) It is mailed free of charge to residents of Camhurst.
(B) It focuses mainly on town events.
(C) It maintains a directory of local businesses.
(D) It has redesigned its Web site.

15. What did Ms. Herrera submit to the *Camhurst Herald*?

(A) A petition
(B) A press release
(C) A guest column
(D) A letter to the editor

16. What topic did the newspaper's March 29 article discuss?

(A) A new downtown traffic pattern
(B) An increase in the number of retail businesses
(C) Local government elections
(D) Proposed new zoning regulations

17. What is suggested about Ms. Herrera's submission?

(A) It presents a well-reasoned viewpoint.
(B) It exceeds the maximum length.
(C) It will be published online only.
(D) It was sent to the wrong person.

18. Why did Mr. Shen write to Ms. Herrera?

(A) To ask her to correct a mistake
(B) To ask her to subscribe to the *Camhurst Herald*
(C) To invite her to become a staff writer
(D) To explain a delay in publishing her submission

Section

8

Section 8 の正解数		
1 回目	2 回目	3 回目
月　日　　　問／19 問	月　日　　　問／19 問	月　日　　　問／19 問

Part 5

□ 1. Passengers are ------- required to present their tickets before boarding the train.

    (A) rather than
    (B) usually
    (C) among
    (D) have to be

□ 2. In January, a restaurant will be opening in the lobby, offering delicious meals and a ------- atmosphere.

    (A) charming
    (B) charmingly
    (C) charmer
    (D) charms

□ 3. The hiring coordinator is ------- disappointed by the small number of applicants for the junior editor position.

    (A) justified
    (B) justifiably
    (C) justifying
    (D) justifiable

□ 4. A major ------- of the shopping center's design was the lack of adequate parking space.

    (A) category
    (B) portion
    (C) shortcoming
    (D) responsibility

□ 5. Dr. Ito will explore preservation methods that are less costly than ------- proposed by the technicians yesterday.

    (A) enough
    (B) itself
    (C) those
    (D) fewer

□ 6. ------- donors significantly increase their pledges will Citizens Dentistry Clinic be able to meet its goals.

    (A) In case
    (B) Even
    (C) Only if
    (D) Except

□ 7. Because their target markets differ, regional sales representatives work ------- of the in-house sales department.

    (A) independently
    (B) enthusiastically
    (C) proficiently
    (D) successfully

Part 6

Questions 8-11 refer to the following letter.

5 January

Dear Employees:

On behalf of the board of directors of Daville Ltd., I am proud to announce our acquisition of GPD Oil and Gas. ------- . The merger of the two companies ------- to result in over $1 billion in
8.   **9.**
cost savings as administrative departments are streamlined.

One major change brought by the merger will be the ------- of the Baker refinery near Melbourne.
10.
All employees currently assigned to that location will be transferred to other facilities.

------- , refining will be increased in our existing New Zealand and UAE facilities. More details
11.
will be provided soon. Please know that we appreciate your hard work, which led to this exciting
opportunity.

Sincerely,

Johnson B. Falworth
Secretary, Board of Directors
Daville Ltd.

---

8. (A) GPD Oil and Gas recently celebrated
        its fortieth anniversary.
    (B) Daville Ltd. is now the region's
        largest distributor of oil and natural
        gas.
    (C) We appreciate your interest in
        investing in our company.
    (D) A new board of directors is elected
        every three years.

9. (A) projects
    (B) projecting
    (C) is projected
    (D) has been projecting

10. (A) closing
    (B) purchase
    (C) dedication
    (D) construction

11. (A) In effect
    (B) In addition
    (C) In case
    (D) In a way

GO ON TO THE NEXT PAGE ⟶

Questions 12-14 refer to the following article.

Banking and Legal Industries Fuel Stiedemann's

LONDON (22 April)—The first year in business has been a very good one for Stiedemann's. — [1] —. Since opening on Rye Street last April, the furniture retailer has reported sales of nearly £2 million. — [2] —.

Much of this success has been driven by bulk purchases of office desks and chairs by nearby banks and law firms. According to Stiedemann's owner, Michaelina Lin, office items accounted for half the store's sales, which is unusual in the industry. — [3] —.

Ms. Lin expects these sales to slow over the next six months, since offices tend to replace desks only after five years or more. Consequently, Stiedemann's will spend the next two years vigorously advertising its inventory of home furnishings.

"We will continue to expand our efforts to attract residential customers," Ms. Lin said. — [4] —.

12. What kind of business is Stiedemann's?

    (A) A bank

    (B) A law firm

    (C) A furniture store

    (D) A real estate broker

13. About how long has Stiedemann's been in business?

    (A) Six months

    (B) One year

    (C) Two years

    (D) Five years

14. In which of the positions marked [1], [2], [3], and [4] does the following sentence best belong?

"Typically, such products represent a quarter of all sales."

    (A) [1]

    (B) [2]

    (C) [3]

    (D) [4]

GO ON TO THE NEXT PAGE $\longrightarrow$

Vendors: Reserve Your Space for the Barbados International Trade Fair!

Saturday and Sunday, September 14–15   **Bridgetown Convention Centre**

The Barbados International Trade Fair returns this year, with several noteworthy changes. We are adding a second day and moving to a new location that offers more space for vendors. Additionally, instead of assigned locations, vendors can now select their preferred exhibit booth. Vendors who reserve by July 1 will receive a 25 percent discount. Reserve your space today!

The Barbados International Trade Fair is the area's primary showcase for locally sourced and produced products. As always, booths are open only to vendors based in Barbados and other Caribbean islands. Our goal is to open up a global market for Caribbean goods. Vendors are invited to mingle with buyers from around the world at an opening reception to be held on Friday night. There is no need to confirm attendance; all exhibitors are invited.

Barbados International Trade Fair Vendor Booth Reservation Form

Company Name: Shade Tree Crafts   **Date:** June 30
Contact Name: Narissa Simpson   **E-mail:** nsimpson@shadetreecrafts.bb

Day(s) You Wish to Exhibit: ☑ Saturday   ☑ Sunday

Preferred Exhibit Space:
Provide back-up choices in case your preferred space is not available.

First choice: Booth 89C
Second choice: Booth 34A
Third choice: Booth 39B
Fourth choice: Booth 75A

A map of all available exhibit spaces can be found on our Web site: www.barbadositf.bb/vendormap.

```
┌──────────────────────────────────────────────────────────────────┐
│                            *E-mail*                                │
├──────────────────────────────────────────────────────────────────┤
│  From:     │ Winston Daley, Barbados International Trade Fair       │
│  To:       │ Narissa Simpson, Shade Tree Crafts                    │
│  Date:     │ August 17                                             │
│  Subject:  │ Your reservation                                      │
├──────────────────────────────────────────────────────────────────┤
│  Dear Ms. Simpson,                                                 │
│                                                                    │
│  Thank you for participating in the Barbados International Trade    │
│  Fair. We have reserved your second-choice selection for the       │
│  event, as your first choice was already taken.                    │
│                                                                    │
│  Consider taking advantage of the opportunity to call attention to │
│  your company by sponsoring a refreshment break. Sponsors' names   │
│  will appear prominently in the program and on signage in the      │
│  break room. For details and pricing, visit our Web site and click │
│  the Sponsorship link.                                             │
│                                                                    │
│  We look forward to seeing you at the event.                       │
│                                                                    │
│  Regards,                                                          │
│                                                                    │
│  Winston Daley                                                     │
│  Fair Coordinator                                                  │
└──────────────────────────────────────────────────────────────────┘
```

15. What does the advertisement suggest will remain unchanged about the fair this year?

(A) The size of the venue
(B) The ways that booths are assigned
(C) The vendors that are invited
(D) The length of the event

16. What is indicated in the advertisement about the reception?

(A) It requires guests to confirm attendance.
(B) It includes performances from Caribbean artists.
(C) It will be held on September 13.
(D) It will be attended by vendors from around the world.

17. What can be concluded about Ms. Simpson?

(A) She will receive a discount on her booth.
(B) She attended the fair last year.
(C) She will miss one of the exhibit days.
(D) She forgot to submit some information.

18. Where will Shade Tree Crafts display its products?

(A) In Booth 34A
(B) In Booth 39B
(C) In Booth 75A
(D) In Booth 89C

19. In the e-mail, what does Mr. Daley encourage Ms. Simpson to do?

(A) Serve refreshments at her booth
(B) Invite competitors to the fair
(C) Become a sponsor
(D) Send him a list of products she sells

Section

9

Part 5

1. Ms. Park received a package in the mail ------- her former boss at Roydon Electric.
   - (A) at
   - (B) from
   - (C) without
   - (D) since

2. All flight ------- and hotel reservations must be made through our partner travel agency, Storg Group.
   - (A) arrangements
   - (B) arranges
   - (C) to arrange
   - (D) will arrange

3. The office picnic planned for this Sunday must be relocated indoors ------- rain is expected.
   - (A) therefore
   - (B) however
   - (C) otherwise
   - (D) because

4. Perry Bank customers will have limited access to ------- online accounts while the Web site is upgraded on May 14.
   - (A) their
   - (B) them
   - (C) they
   - (D) themselves

5. Guests ------- at the Maramigo Hotel can use a mobile phone app to rate the hotel's service.
   - (A) describing
   - (B) planned
   - (C) staying
   - (D) returned

6. The budget legislation ------- by Ms. Ramirez' committee includes funding for repairs to the Fencher Bridge.
   - (A) occurred
   - (B) passed
   - (C) relaxed
   - (D) told

7. ------- the office chairs were delivered today, the new desks will not arrive until Monday.
   - (A) Once
   - (B) Next
   - (C) Although
   - (D) Unlike

Part 6

Questions 8-11 refer to the following e-mail.

To: m.tennyson@yackelartmuseum.co.uk
From: l.rivera@pollimail.co.uk
Date: Monday, 9 March
Subject: Re: Onboarding
Attachment: Rivera_Bio

Dear Ms. Tennyson:

I just completed the new-hire procedures online, but there may be an issue. When I hit the submit button, the screen went blank briefly, and I was returned to the main page. I never got a confirmation message of any kind. Can you please verify that my ------- was received?
8.

I am also attaching the staff biography you asked me ------- for the Web site. I tried my best to
9.
follow the format you provided. ------- . Now that I am looking at everyone else's, I see that it
10.
might be too different from the others. Please let me know if I should ------- it.
11.

Kind regards,

Liam Rivera

8. (A) gift
(B) approval
(C) payment
(D) information

9. (A) to write
(B) writing it
(C) that wrote
(D) was written

10. (A) I greatly appreciate their help.
(B) Likewise, I will see what I can do.
(C) However, I also wanted to add some of my personality.
(D) I believe it can be found somewhere online.

11. (A) borrow
(B) revise
(C) locate
(D) protect

GO ON TO THE NEXT PAGE ⟶

Part 7

Questions 12-13 refer to the following text-message chain.

Julio Sanchez [4:02 P.M.]
I think we're going to have to postpone the meeting tomorrow morning.

Sonia McCauley [4:04 P.M.]
We can't! We need it to prepare for the conference.

Julio Sanchez [4:06 P.M.]
Well, Mr. Nassar just called me. His flight was delayed, and he won't be back until late tomorrow night.

Sonia McCauley [4:08 P.M.]
Guess what—I just got a text from Ellen Keskinen. She's giving a presentation to clients tomorrow morning. She isn't available until the afternoon, and I'm booked then. We all really need to meet, though.

Julio Sanchez [4:12 P.M.]
The conference is on Friday afternoon. We'll be traveling on Friday morning, so Friday won't work.

Sonia McCauley [4:13 P.M.]
Let's see. It's already Tuesday afternoon now. What about Thursday? Same time.

Julio Sanchez [4:14 P.M.]
I'll check everyone's calendars.

12. Why must Ms. McCauley and Mr. Sanchez have a meeting?

(A) To plan for an event

(B) To respond to an unexpected request

(C) To select staff for a new project

(D) To prepare for a client visit

13. At 4:13 P.M., what does Ms. McCauley imply when she writes, "Same time"?

(A) She realizes the meeting will conflict with a conference.

(B) She is concerned that Ms. Keskinen will not be available to meet.

(C) She would like the group to meet in the morning on Thursday.

(D) She thinks the meeting will last for one hour.

GO ON TO THE NEXT PAGE ⟶

https://www.calgaryrenewalcentre.ca/about

At the Calgary Renewal Centre (CRC), our mission ever since our founding a decade ago has been to improve our community by repairing and restoring historic buildings and structures. We want residents and visitors to be able to wander down our streets and learn about our cultural, social, and architectural history. We are fortunate to bring together volunteers from around the region to assist in different areas of our work. Some volunteers help with administrative tasks in our office on Euclid Street; some reach out to private organizations that donate money and materials; some contribute their expertise in renovation practices or regional history; and still others assist our builders and carpenters at our work sites. Our partnership with Hanselka University's School of Architecture has opened up additional volunteer opportunities for those with a background in building design.

We are always pleased to welcome teams of volunteers from local companies, schools, and community groups. To arrange a group volunteer shift, submit the Volunteer Roster form at calgaryrenewalcentre.ca/volunteerform. On this form, indicate your group's desired date and time to volunteer and the type of work your group would like to do. For more information, contact our volunteer coordinator, Gerald Knoller, at knoller@calgaryrenewalcentre.ca.

Calgary Renewal Centre Volunteer Roster

Name of company/organization/school: BRH Technologies
Application date: 10 July
Preferred volunteer date/time: 12 August, 5 P.M.–8 P.M.
Preferred type of work: Administrative

Name	E-mail	Previous CRC volunteer experience?	Signed CRC liability waiver? (All volunteers must sign a liability waiver before CRC can confirm the shift.)
Moira Beaulieu	mbeaulieu@brh.ca	Y	Y
Jay Anish	janish@brh.ca	N	Y
Brad Mitsui	bmitsui@brh.ca	N	N
Anika Klum	aklum@brh.ca	Y	Y
Nigel Macomber	nmacomber@brh.ca	Y	Y

From:	Alana Moncrief <moncrief@calgaryrenewalcentre.ca>
To:	Gerald Knoller <knoller@calgaryrenewalcentre.ca>
Subject:	Please follow up
Date:	31 July

Hi Gerald,

I am reviewing the paperwork for the groups scheduled to volunteer with us in August. I see that a piece of paperwork for one of the BRH Technologies' team members is missing. This needs to be submitted before the group can visit us. Please follow up as soon as possible.

Thank you,

Alana Moncrief
Director, Community Engagement

☐ **14.** According to the Web page, in what area are CRC's efforts focused?

(A) Street and walkway repair
(B) Environmental sustainability
(C) Historic preservation
(D) Cultural diversity

☐ **15.** What does the Web page indicate about CRC?

(A) It was founded by a university professor.
(B) It has been operating for ten years.
(C) It is funded by grants from the government.
(D) It will soon merge with another organization.

☐ **16.** Where will the group from BRH Technologies most likely go on August 12?

(A) To Hanselka University
(B) To an office on Euclid Street
(C) To a donor organization's headquarters
(D) To a construction site

☐ **17.** What does the form indicate about Ms. Beaulieu?

(A) She works for BRH Technologies as an administrative assistant.
(B) She was selected to be the leader of her volunteer team.
(C) She needs to end her shift early.
(D) She has volunteered with CRC in the past.

☐ **18.** What will Mr. Knoller probably do after receiving the e-mail from Ms. Moncrief?

(A) Move the BRH Technologies shift to an earlier time slot
(B) Reassign Mr. Anish to a different team
(C) Send a reminder e-mail to Mr. Mitsui
(D) Request that BRH Technologies add more people to its team

Section

10

Part 5

☐ **1.** One ------- of working as a flight attendant is being able to travel the world.

    (A) improvement
    (B) benefit
    (C) expedition
    (D) subject

☐ **2.** Q-pert Cable Company announced plans to expand its services to over 40,000 ------- businesses.

    (A) add
    (B) additional
    (C) adding
    (D) additionally

☐ **3.** The TKM Network will be turning Mr. Zhao's book into a television series to be broadcast ------- in December.

    (A) really
    (B) exactly
    (C) already
    (D) early

☐ **4.** Extra books of blank invoice forms will be ordered ------- sales representatives attend the trade fair.

    (A) before
    (B) either
    (C) whereas
    (D) whether

☐ **5.** As project manager, Mr. Jeong has been tasked with ------- reviewing all new construction plans.

    (A) careful
    (B) more careful
    (C) carefulness
    (D) carefully

☐ **6.** ------- its newly opened plant, Buhr Concrete is now the largest employer in the region.

    (A) When
    (B) Until
    (C) As if
    (D) With

☐ **7.** The monthly payment plan might be the ------- option for many consumers.

    (A) affordability
    (B) affording
    (C) most affordable
    (D) more affordably

Part 6

Questions 8-11 refer to the following advertisement.

Going Native Xeriscaping

Low-Water Garden Experts

Xeriscaping is a type of garden design that uses native plants that can thrive in your garden with very little ------- . Using drought-resistant plants helps ------- conserve limited water resources.
8. **9.**
Less water used means lower utility bills. And with so many beautiful native plants to choose from, anyone can enjoy a garden full of vibrant colors and interesting textures while ------- water use.
10.

Going Native has been creating xeriscapes for 20 years. ------- . Call today for a free consultation.
11.

---

8. (A) soil
   (B) sunlight
   (C) fertilizer
   (D) moisture

9. (A) him
   (B) you
   (C) them
   (D) itself

10. (A) reducing
   (B) to reduce
   (C) they reduced
   (D) the reduction of

11. (A) However, we appreciate your request for native plants.
   (B) Similarly, roses are available in many different colors.
   (C) A backyard swimming pool can be fun for the whole family.
   (D) Our experienced designers can create the garden of your dreams.

GO ON TO THE NEXT PAGE ⟶

Part 7

Questions 12-15 refer to the following e-mail.

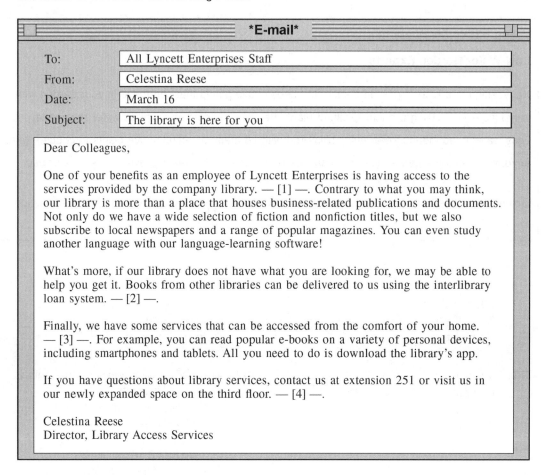

E-mail

To: All Lyncett Enterprises Staff

From: Celestina Reese

Date: March 16

Subject: The library is here for you

Dear Colleagues,

One of your benefits as an employee of Lyncett Enterprises is having access to the services provided by the company library. — [1] —. Contrary to what you may think, our library is more than a place that houses business-related publications and documents. Not only do we have a wide selection of fiction and nonfiction titles, but we also subscribe to local newspapers and a range of popular magazines. You can even study another language with our language-learning software!

What's more, if our library does not have what you are looking for, we may be able to help you get it. Books from other libraries can be delivered to us using the interlibrary loan system. — [2] —.

Finally, we have some services that can be accessed from the comfort of your home. — [3] —. For example, you can read popular e-books on a variety of personal devices, including smartphones and tablets. All you need to do is download the library's app.

If you have questions about library services, contact us at extension 251 or visit us in our newly expanded space on the third floor. — [4] —.

Celestina Reese
Director, Library Access Services

12. According to the e-mail, what is a service offered by the library?

(A) Access to language-learning materials

(B) Subscriptions to foreign newspapers

(C) Training workshops for employees

(D) Space for employees to host events

13. Why does Ms. Reese mention the library's app?

(A) To explain an increase in fees

(B) To call attention to a technical issue

(C) To announce some changes being made by the library

(D) To describe how employees can access e-books

14. What does Ms. Reese indicate about the library?

(A) Its space was recently enlarged.

(B) It will soon change its operating hours.

(C) It allows employees to borrow electronic devices.

(D) Its librarians all work part-time.

15. In which of the positions marked [1], [2], [3], and [4] does the following sentence best belong?

"It takes just two days."

(A) [1]

(B) [2]

(C) [3]

(D) [4]

Section

10

GO ON TO THE NEXT PAGE ⟶

Fronteras and Company

We have all of your family's fashion needs!

October Special Sales

Valid in store and online. Receive discounts online using the discount codes below.

10% off Dresses
Use Code: OCTFORM71

20% off all Accessories (excluding hats)
Use Code: OCTACC43

30% off Children's Wear
Use Code: OCTCHIL29

Free reusable shopping bag included with orders over $75! Only one discount code can be applied per order.

From:	Ameena Almasi <aalmasi@rhyta.com.au>
To:	Fronteras and Company Customer Service <custserv@fronteras.com.au>
Date:	Tuesday, 16 October 6:44 A.M.
Subject:	Order discount code

Hello,

I just now attempted to place an online order for 3 boys' shirts on your Web site. However, when I tried to enter the discount code, I received an error message saying that the code was invalid. I tried three times to make sure that I was entering the code correctly. Can you help me with this? I would really like to order the shirts today to get them before 20 October, which is the date of a child's birthday party.

Thank you,

Ameena Almasi

From:	Fronteras and Company Customer Service <custserv@fronteras.com.au>
To:	Ameena Almasi <aalmasi@rhyta.com.au>
Date:	Tuesday, 16 October 11:04 A.M.
Subject:	RE: Order discount code

Dear Ms. Almasi,

Thank you for your e-mail. I am sorry to hear about your problem ordering on our Web site. I did some research and found that the wrong code was included in the advertisement. We apologize for the inconvenience. We have fixed the problem, and the code in the advertisement will now be accepted.

Because this was entirely our fault, I have arranged for express shipping at no extra charge. You can expect to receive your order one day before the party you mentioned.

If you have any other problems or questions, please don't hesitate to write or call our customer service line.

Sincerely,

Sheldon Blythe
Fronteras and Company Customer Service Representative

16. What kind of business is Fronteras and Company?

(A) A clothing store
(B) An advertising agency
(C) A party planning company
(D) An electronics store

17. How can a customer qualify for a free bag?

(A) By responding to a survey
(B) By spending a minimum amount
(C) By placing an order before October 15
(D) By signing up for a loyalty program

18. How much of a discount did Ms. Almasi expect to receive on her order?

(A) 5 percent
(B) 10 percent
(C) 20 percent
(D) 30 percent

19. Why did Ms. Almasi have a problem with her order?

(A) Because the store did not have the item
(B) Because too many people were using the Web site
(C) Because there was an error in an advertisement
(D) Because a piece of equipment was damaged

20. When will Ms. Almasi most likely receive her order?

(A) On October 16
(B) On October 17
(C) On October 19
(D) On October 20

Section

11

Part 5

☐ **1.** The CEO addressed the board members, ------- were not expecting him to announce his retirement.

    (A) which
    (B) whose
    (C) what
    (D) who

☐ **2.** To be considered for the editor -------, applicants must submit a résumé by Friday.

    (A) case
    (B) remedy
    (C) position
    (D) attitude

☐ **3.** Steinhart and Sons' ------- showed a steep decline in the previous quarter.

    (A) earnings
    (B) earn
    (C) earned
    (D) earns

☐ **4.** ------- in our company is welcome to attend the demonstration of our new product.

    (A) Those
    (B) Anyone
    (C) One another
    (D) Whichever

☐ **5.** Local office workers like Vasalisa's Café for its quick service and ------- priced food.

    (A) economic
    (B) economize
    (C) economies
    (D) economically

☐ **6.** The Argenca Company's new pricing plan is a ------- move to attract more customers.

    (A) strategic
    (B) preventable
    (C) distant
    (D) previous

☐ **7.** All payments must be checked ------- to ensure that they comply with tax rules.

    (A) eagerly
    (B) commonly
    (C) thoroughly
    (D) nearly

Part 6

Questions 8-11 refer to the following article.

Rite Shop Stores Introduce New Collaborations

National grocery chain Rite Shop has just announced partnerships with several specialty food brands ------- for their unique products. These include Gerry's Cheeses, H&R Bagels, and Daily
    8.
Bread baked goods. The brands will ------- be available at select Rite Shop stores. ------- .
    9.   **10.**

"I think customers will be really pleased to see these brands at Rite Shop," CEO Natalie Yalbirs said at a press conference on Wednesday. "And we at Rite Shop are excited about this opportunity to expand our ------- ."
    11.

☐ **8.** (A) known
        (B) that know
        (C) they know
        (D) were known

☐ **9.** (A) still
        (B) soon
        (C) likewise
        (D) ever

☐ **10.** (A) Nevertheless, hot coffee can now be purchased at all stores.
        (B) Rite Shop was founded more than 25 years ago.
        (C) All stores will begin selling the products over the next several months.
        (D) For example, Daily Bread operates locally.

☐ **11.** (A) budget
        (B) offerings
        (C) warehouse
        (D) membership

GO ON TO THE NEXT PAGE ⟶

Part 7

Questions 12-15 refer to the following text-message chain.

Annabelle Marder (11:12 A.M.) Hi, Preeti and Kwesi. I'd like to know if the organizing committee of the Cultural Heritage Festival is still interested in contracting my band for the event.

Preeti Sandhu (11:15 A.M.) Hi, Annabelle. I believe we are, but maybe Kwesi can confirm that. This time he's in charge of booking the artists, not me.

Annabelle Marder (11:17 A.M.) I understand, but I'd appreciate a response soon. We're working on a new album and there's an open spot at the recording studio the weekend of June 26.

Preeti Sandhu (11:18 A.M.) Which is when we have our event. I see.

Kwesi Asiamah (11:20 A.M.) Hi, Annabelle! I've been meaning to contact you. We are very much interested, actually. Your band was a major draw at the festival two years ago. We missed your unique mix of salsa and reggae music last year.

Preeti Sandhu (11:24 A.M.) Yes, it's too bad you couldn't make it.

Annabelle Marder (11:25 A.M.) If I'm remembering correctly, we had another commitment we couldn't get out of. We were disappointed about it, too.

Kwesi Asiamah (11:26 A.M.) Well, once I've confirmed the performance schedule, I'll send you all the relevant information. Is tomorrow good enough?

Annabelle Marder (11:27 A.M.) Tomorrow's fine. It gives me time to work with the studio to find another available slot. Looking forward to hearing from you.

12. What is indicated about Ms. Marder?

    (A) She is concerned about a scheduling conflict.

    (B) She is responsible for hiring festival performers.

    (C) She is on the festival's organizing committee.

    (D) She is working on writing a book.

13. What is NOT suggested about the Cultural Heritage Festival?

    (A) It features live music.

    (B) It will be held in June.

    (C) It takes place every year.

    (D) It requires tickets for entry.

14. At 11:24 A.M., what does Ms. Sandhu mean when she writes, "it's too bad you couldn't make it"?

    (A) Transportation to an event was unavailable.

    (B) A studio recording session was canceled.

    (C) She is sorry that Ms. Marder's band missed an event.

    (D) She wishes Ms. Marder's band still played reggae music.

15. What does Mr. Asiamah promise to do?

    (A) Contact the studio

    (B) Provide more details

    (C) Meet with Ms. Marder

    (D) Update a contract

GO ON TO THE NEXT PAGE $\longrightarrow$

Proposal: Hoek Co. Community Garden Project

Summary: As part of our ongoing community outreach programme, Hoek Co. is sponsoring a community garden in the Ostend neighborhood, close to our warehouse location. We have hired landscape architect Todor Jansen to design the space, but company volunteers will build the garden's structures. See below for a preliminary budget for the garden's raised beds.

Quantity	Item	Cost (per unit)
24	3-metre length boards	€12.25
24	4-metre length boards	€15.75
3	Box 20 cm nails	€8.50
16	Metal corner braces	€2.99
16	2-metre wood corner posts	€10.00

Ostend Community Garden
Volunteer Schedule (Team 1)

- Weekend 1 (18–19 March): Clear brush; level ground
- Weekend 2 (25–26 March): Construct wood planting-bed frames; place frames in specified locations
- Weekend 3 (1–2 April): Install soil and fertilizer; plant first seeds
- Weekend 4 (8–9 April): Water and weed seedlings; establish garden care schedule for Team 2

Ostend Community Garden Map
(with planting start dates)

Bed 1
Lettuce (1 April)
Peas (15 April)

Bed 2
Strawberries (15 April)
Blueberries (29 April)

Bed 3
Squash (3 June)
Sprouts (10 June)

Bed 4
Corn (1 July)
Beans (15 July)

16. Where will the community garden be located?

(A) Inside a city park
(B) Across from an office building
(C) Next to a factory
(D) Near a storage facility

17. According to the proposal, how many corner posts are needed to build the raised beds?

(A) 4
(B) 16
(C) 20
(D) 24

18. By when will Hoek Co. need to purchase the materials in the budget?

(A) Weekend 1
(B) Weekend 2
(C) Weekend 3
(D) Weekend 4

19. What will the Team 1 volunteers plant in the garden?

(A) Lettuce
(B) Peas
(C) Corn
(D) Squash

20. According to the map, where will garden volunteers plant two kinds of fruit?

(A) In Bed 1
(B) In Bed 2
(C) In Bed 3
(D) In Bed 4

Section

12

Part 5

1. The retirement party for Ms. Iashvili will take place at Blue Marina Grill, a ------- restaurant on the waterfront.

(A) popular
(B) tentative
(C) multiple
(D) continual

2. Cardenas Industries requests your patience and ------- as we introduce our new payment system.

(A) cooperate
(B) cooperated
(C) cooperation
(D) cooperatively

3. Mr. Wong had ------- accepted the job offer but later declined it for unspecified reasons.

(A) provision
(B) provisions
(C) provisionally
(D) provisional

4. One of Ms. Lampron's responsibilities at the child-care facility is to ------- the schedule for the staff.

(A) educate
(B) permit
(C) invest
(D) create

5. Paint manufacturing involves the mixing of a number of raw materials ------- various proportions.

(A) on
(B) in
(C) after
(D) over

6. Mr. Selman is expected to leave for Istanbul on May 24 and ------- on May 30.

(A) has returned
(B) returning
(C) return
(D) be returned

7. Villadsen mobile phones come with a two-year guarantee against breakage ------- the standard manufacturer's warranty.

(A) on top of
(B) ahead of
(C) in case of
(D) near to

Part 6

Questions 8-11 refer to the following memo.

From: Sergio L. McGovern, Vice President of Operations
To: All Floor Supervisors
Subject: Inspections
Date: 3 June

As part of our efforts ------- product quality and ensure compliance with national regulations, all
      8.

manufacturing units will be subject to random inspections effective immediately. These checks

------- conducted by engineers from Venturia Systems, Inc. They will monitor the production line
  9.

and observe warehouse operations. Please be aware that the inspectors will arrive without

------- . Thus, they may walk in at any time. We ask that you proceed as usual with your work
 10.

while the inspectors complete theirs. Within one week of each inspection, a detailed report will be

sent directly to me. ------- . Thank you.
            11.

□ **8.** (A) improving
(B) to improve
(C) that improved
(D) of improvement

□ **9.** (A) were
(B) will be
(C) had been
(D) were being

□ **10.** (A) warning
(B) delay
(C) permission
(D) accommodation

□ **11.** (A) Please submit your evaluation upon completion.
(B) Please arrive promptly at the agreed-upon time.
(C) Inspectors will register at the front desk.
(D) You will be receiving a copy as well.

GO ON TO THE NEXT PAGE ⟶

Section **12**

Part 7

Questions 12-13 refer to the following article.

Tiff Creek Update

CORDALE (April 30)—The area around Tiff Creek, long an eyesore to commuters on the West Valley train line, is in the final stage of restoration before its scheduled opening on July 1 as a nature park.

This week marks the two-year anniversary of approval of the project, although work did not commence until January. The area was previously home to an industrial glass factory.

Cordale mayor Ed Scala announced today that workers are expected to complete the planting of native grasses by June. Workers have already removed old concrete and asphalt, cleaned out the creek, and replaced existing soil with sand.

□ **12.** When did the restoration work begin?

    (A) In January

    (B) In April

    (C) In June

    (D) In July

□ **13.** According to the article, what will happen next?

    (A) A factory will be repaired.

    (B) Grasses will be planted.

    (C) A train station will be completed.

    (D) Soil will be replaced.

Section

12

GO ON TO THE NEXT PAGE $\longrightarrow$

Cobh, Co. Cork (15 February)—The town of Cobh will host its first-ever community fair on Saturday, 28 April. According to the organisers, the fair will feature businesses and community organisations not only from Cobh but also from the surrounding towns along Cork Harbour. The event will be free to the public, and booths will be clustered in three central locations around town.

"One of our goals is to get people to stop by all of the special places our town has to offer," says event coordinator Caoimhe Carroll. "Informational booths on local businesses and services will be set up outside the Cobh Sculpture Park, food vendors will be in the parking lot of the nearby Cobh Music Hall, and art vendors will be scattered along the harbour. We want people to enjoy exploring the area."

Vendors interested in participating can apply at www.cobhcommunityfair.ie. Those who register before April will receive a gift tote bag with coupons for area businesses.

Please tell us about your experience as a vendor at the Cobh Community Fair!

Name: _Joanna Harbro_

Business Name: _Joabro Jewellery_

I registered as soon as the news article about the fair was published because I was so excited to be a part of this event! I really enjoyed chatting with visitors, and I sold much of my inventory! However, I think visitors were expecting more artists to participate. Additional outreach and advertising before the next fair would likely get more of us involved.

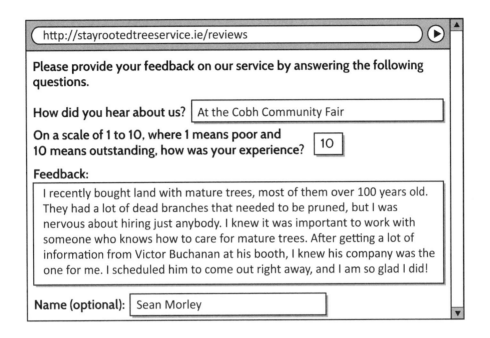

http://stayrootedtreeservice.ie/reviews

Please provide your feedback on our service by answering the following questions.

How did you hear about us? At the Cobh Community Fair

On a scale of 1 to 10, where 1 means poor and 10 means outstanding, how was your experience? 10

Feedback:

I recently bought land with mature trees, most of them over 100 years old. They had a lot of dead branches that needed to be pruned, but I was nervous about hiring just anybody. I knew it was important to work with someone who knows how to care for mature trees. After getting a lot of information from Victor Buchanan at his booth, I knew his company was the one for me. I scheduled him to come out right away, and I am so glad I did!

Name (optional): Sean Morley

☐ **14.** According to the article, why did fair organizers place vendors in different areas?

(A) To promote exercise
(B) To encourage sightseeing
(C) To minimize traffic congestion
(D) To accommodate parking limitations

☐ **15.** What is implied about Ms. Harbro?

(A) She received a gift for registering early.
(B) She qualified for a discounted registration fee.
(C) She was featured in a news article.
(D) She was able to choose the location of her booth.

☐ **16.** In the comment card, what does Ms. Harbro suggest for future events?

(A) Posting clearer signs around the fairgrounds
(B) Recruiting more art vendors
(C) Providing assistance with booth setup
(D) Offering better options for displaying merchandise

☐ **17.** What is implied about Mr. Buchanan?

(A) He organized the fair.
(B) He sold food at the fair.
(C) He commutes to Cobh on Saturdays.
(D) He had a booth outside the Cobh Sculpture Park.

☐ **18.** According to the online review form, what was Mr. Morley's priority?

(A) The ability to provide same-day service
(B) A long history of working locally
(C) Experience with caring for older trees
(D) A willingness to take away cut branches

Section
12

Section

13

Section 13 の正解数		
1 回目	2 回目	3 回目
月　日　　問／18問	月　日　　問／18問	月　日　　問／18問

Part 5

1. The Web site for the Thayerton Chamber of Commerce ------- a comprehensive list of all the businesses in town.

   (A) contain
   (B) containing
   (C) contains
   (D) to contain

2. Mr. Paek will discuss the importance ------- courteous customer service.

   (A) to
   (B) at
   (C) by
   (D) of

3. The plans to add a new wing to the building are progressing -------.

   (A) smooth
   (B) smoothness
   (C) smoothing
   (D) smoothly

4. ------- Dr. Barrios is new to the firm, she has already acquired twelve clients for us.

   (A) Whenever
   (B) Although
   (C) After
   (D) Once

5. The new furniture makes a ------- addition to the company's lobby.

   (A) delightful
   (B) delightfully
   (C) delight
   (D) delights

6. To ------- funding from investors, we must show that there is a strong potential market for our products.

   (A) withhold
   (B) desire
   (C) secure
   (D) conduct

7. Mr. Hobrock has a very high ------- for the new Italian restaurant in town.

   (A) regarding
   (B) regard
   (C) regarded
   (D) regards

Part 6

Questions 8-11 refer to the following article.

TARPON SPRINGS, FL (June 24)—For the first time ever, the Tarpon Springs Museum of Art

------- the works of famed local artist Nikos Parios. The retrospective show is planned for the
8.

entire month of July.

Mr. Parios will attend the opening of the show on the evening of July 1. However, not all the works in

the show will be ------- . Works by four younger artists who have studied with Mr. Parios will also
9.

be featured. ------- .
10.

The show will be the first to take place since the museum's recent remodeling. ------- visitors will
11.

notice that the murals on the walls have been restored and a large skylight has been installed.

☐ **8.** (A) has exhibited
　　(B) exhibit
　　(C) will exhibit
　　(D) exhibited

☐ **9.** (A) its
　　(B) his
　　(C) hers
　　(D) theirs

☐ **10.** (A) Mr. Parios began painting at a young age.
　　(B) The artists will join Mr. Parios on July 1.
　　(C) Mr. Parios was born in Tarpon Springs.
　　(D) One mural was painted by Mr. Parios.

☐ **11.** (A) Preceding
　　(B) Early
　　(C) Official
　　(D) Regular

Section

13

GO ON TO THE NEXT PAGE ──────→

109

Part 7

Questions 12-13 refer to the following text-message chain.

Shekeia Jacobs (9:04 A.M.)
Hello. I called into the video conference, but no one else was on the line. When the meeting date was changed, was the phone number or dial-in code also changed?

Karl Rudd (9:05 A.M.)
It's today at 10. It was previously scheduled for 9, but when we changed the date, we also moved the start time. I'm sorry that I forgot to send you the update.

Shekeia Jacobs (9:07 A.M.)
It's fine. Is the dial-in information the same?

Karl Rudd (9:08 A.M.)
Yes.

Shekeia Jacobs (9:09 A.M.)
Thanks. I am just glad I didn't miss it. See you on the call soon!

□ **12.** Why did Ms. Jacobs contact Mr. Rudd?

    (A) To give him a recommendation

    (B) To change a dial-in code

    (C) To inquire about a meeting

    (D) To cancel a video call

□ **13.** At 9:07 A.M., what does Ms. Jacobs most likely mean when she writes, "It's fine"?

    (A) A new time is acceptable to her.

    (B) The list of participants is final.

    (C) She approves of the location for a meeting.

    (D) She likes some updated phone equipment.

GO ON TO THE NEXT PAGE ———————→

Questions 14-18 refer to the following e-mail and chart.

```
╔══════════════════════════ *E-mail* ══════════════════════════╗
```

To:	Department Deans
From:	Dorit Perez, Director, University Library System
Date:	May 02
Subject:	Laptop computer kiosks
Attachment:	📎 Location chart

As you all know by now, the automated laptop checkout kiosk that was installed about one year ago in the Shelburne University Library has been popular with students. This main library kiosk offers an easy and secure way to access laptop computers 24 hours a day. As long as a student is officially enrolled in a university program, the checkout equipment simply reads the chip in the student's ID card and dispenses the laptop from its lockbox. Staff members at the library circulation desk can attend to other duties because they no longer need to assist students with a lengthy checkout process.

Because of our success, we have decided to expand this concept to other locations on campus beginning the end of this month. As the chart suggests, the laptop inventory at the additional self-help kiosks will vary in number based on anticipated use. Please note that the last location listed is tentative, pending Facilities Department budget approval. It will likely be operational late next month.

Please contact me with any questions or concerns.

Kiosk Location Description	Hours of Operation	Laptop Capacity
Student Plaza	8:00 A.M. – 10:00 P.M.	20
Health Sciences Center	8:00 A.M. – 6:00 P.M.	20
Engineering School	8:00 A.M. – 6:00 P.M.	36
Institute of Business and Industry	8:00 A.M. – 10:00 P.M.	30
Department of Languages	10:00 A.M. – 5:00 P.M.	15

14. What action was taken by Shelburne University last year?

(A) The hiring of additional library staff
(B) The simplification of a checkout process
(C) The creation of classrooms in a library
(D) The opening of a new campus

15. What is indicated about the kiosk in the university library?

(A) It can be used to return books.
(B) It is next to the circulation desk.
(C) It is accessible 24 hours a day.
(D) It is not functioning properly.

16. In the e-mail, the phrase "attend to" in paragraph 1, line 6, is closest in meaning to

(A) take care of
(B) get along with
(C) wait on
(D) appeal to

17. What does the chart suggest about the kiosk at the Engineering School?

(A) It will open in June.
(B) It is far from the campus center.
(C) It will offer two laptop models.
(D) It is expected to be relatively popular.

18. What does Ms. Perez expect the Facilities Department to approve?

(A) A kiosk at the Department of Languages
(B) Improved security measures for kiosks
(C) Expanded hours of operation
(D) Updated student ID cards

Section

14

Section 14 の正解数		
1回目	2回目	3回目
月　　日　　　問／18問	月　　日　　　問／18問	月　　日　　　問／18問

Part 5

□ **1.** Mr. Tran sent the pamphlet back to the printers because the page ------- were incorrect.

    (A) users
    (B) powers
    (C) timers
    (D) numbers

□ **2.** Ms. Becker was chosen for the position of vice president because of her ------- ability to lead.

    (A) nature
    (B) natural
    (C) naturally
    (D) naturalness

□ **3.** The Amsel Plumbing Company is doing well ------- some changes in management.

    (A) inside
    (B) despite
    (C) opposite
    (D) underneath

□ **4.** The media consulting firm Greensap Group can ------- solutions for your business outreach challenges.

    (A) provide
    (B) provider
    (C) provision
    (D) provided

□ **5.** Tramont Builders uses construction materials of the ------- quality.

    (A) highest
    (B) improved
    (C) attractive
    (D) positive

□ **6.** On the day before a holiday, Ms. Pham ------- allows her employees to leave an hour early.

    (A) generalize
    (B) generalization
    (C) general
    (D) generally

□ **7.** Retail managers in regions with cold winters often notice a ------- in sales during the season.

    (A) term
    (B) drop
    (C) trade
    (D) ride

Part 6

Questions 8-11 refer to the following memo.

To: All employees
From: Martha Bauer
Subject: Meetings
Date: April 4

In an attempt to improve productivity, we have analyzed the most effective ways to communicate information ------- our company. ------- , we have decided to make an effort to reduce the number
8. **9.**
of meetings held each month. To that end, we now ------- that employees adhere to general
10.
guidelines when scheduling a meeting. These include always writing a detailed agenda for any meeting and expressly stating a specific end time for meetings. In addition, employees should only be invited to meetings if their presence is essential. ------- . By following these guidelines, we
11.
hope that we all will have more time to commit to our work.

8. (A) near
(B) against
(C) following
(D) within

9. (A) As a result
(B) Even so
(C) Meanwhile
(D) Instead

10. (A) asking
(B) asked
(C) asks
(D) ask

11. (A) Tomorrow's meeting will be held in the auditorium.
(B) An updated agenda will be sent separately.
(C) If you do not need to attend, decline the invitation.
(D) If you are available to help, send me an e-mail.

Section
14

Part 7

Questions 12-13 refer to the following e-mail.

	E-mail
To:	Pamela Doan <pameladoan@worldtreasuresshop.co.uk>
From:	Sara Atwater <saraatwater@zolomail.co.uk>
Subject:	Jewelry sales
Date:	5 July

Dear Ms. Doan,

Thank you for meeting with me yesterday to discuss selling my handmade earrings in your World Treasures Shop. I am thrilled that you would consider selling my designs with your other fine merchandise. I can remember saving money from my first part-time job to buy a bracelet there for my mother's birthday.

The consignment arrangement we discussed wherein you would receive 20 percent of the sales price is agreeable to me. I would like to begin our six-month trial period on 1 August. May I come to set up my display that morning about an hour before the shop opens?

Sincerely,

Sara Atwater

12. What is indicated about Ms. Atwater?

    (A) She has previously worked at World Treasures Shop.

    (B) She sells products from World Treasures Shop in her store.

    (C) She is applying for a job at World Treasures Shop.

    (D) She is a former customer of World Treasures Shop.

13. What is Ms. Atwater requesting?

    (A) A time when she can go to the shop

    (B) A 20 percent share of the profits

    (C) An extension of her initial trial period

    (D) A larger display area that she can use

GO ON TO THE NEXT PAGE ⟶

Questions 14-18 refer to the following e-mails.

To:	williamc@sunmail.ca
From:	reservations@goldflagairways.ca
Subject:	Gold Flag Airways–Information
Date:	1 June

SECTION 1: Reservation 849207
Passenger name: William Conners
Frequent flier ID: 36B117

SECTION 2: Flight GF2465
Depart: YVR, Vancouver, BC, Canada
Date/time: 7 June, 14:40
Destination: ICN, Seoul, South Korea
Arrival time: 17:50
Seat: Coach class 28C

SECTION 3: Flight GF3400
Depart: ICN, Seoul, South Korea
Date/time: 12 June, 15:30
Destination: YVR, Vancouver, BC, Canada
Arrival time: 9:20
Seat: Coach class 31A

SECTION 4: Policies
Please review this e-mail carefully for the specifics of your ticket information. Ensure that passenger's name matches exactly as it appears on traveler's identification documents. If any corrections are needed, e-mail us at reservations@goldflagairways.ca. Requests for any changes to this information must be received at least 48 hours in advance of flight time.

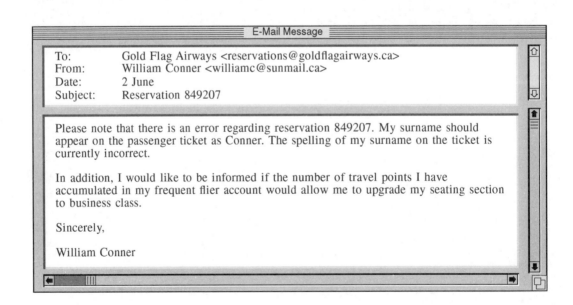

E-Mail Message

To: Gold Flag Airways <reservations@goldflagairways.ca>
From: William Conner <williamc@sunmail.ca>
Date: 2 June
Subject: Reservation 849207

Please note that there is an error regarding reservation 849207. My surname should appear on the passenger ticket as Conner. The spelling of my surname on the ticket is currently incorrect.

In addition, I would like to be informed if the number of travel points I have accumulated in my frequent flier account would allow me to upgrade my seating section to business class.

Sincerely,

William Conner

14. What is the purpose of the first e-mail?

(A) To confirm a frequent flier membership

(B) To promote a new airline

(C) To explain changes to a schedule

(D) To provide the details of a ticket purchase

15. What is implied about Gold Flag Airways?

(A) It charges a fee to change reservation information.

(B) It requires at least 24 hours notice for cancellations.

(C) It offers direct routes between Vancouver and Seoul.

(D) It is popular with budget travelers.

16. What is suggested about Mr. Conner?

(A) He is traveling to a job interview.

(B) He has traveled on Gold Flag Airways in the past.

(C) He would like to request a discount on a ticket.

(D) He has a special luggage request.

17. What section of the first e-mail contains a problem?

(A) Section 1

(B) Section 2

(C) Section 3

(D) Section 4

18. In the second e-mail, the word "informed" in paragraph 2, line 1, is closest in meaning to

(A) notified

(B) proposed

(C) educated

(D) directed

Section

14

Section

15

Part 5

1. ------- to the carpentry apprenticeship will depend on the applicant's previous experience.

    (A) Accept
    (B) Acceptance
    (C) Acceptable
    (D) Acceptably

2. Ms. Nakamoto will be ------- Hwang Industries as its president of operations on Monday.

    (A) joining
    (B) maintaining
    (C) trading
    (D) merging

3. Please note that per store policy, prices on sale items are not -------.

    (A) negotiable
    (B) negotiator
    (C) negotiation
    (D) negotiating

4. In his presentation, Mr. Mennon ------- the strengths and weaknesses of the proposal.

    (A) contained
    (B) outlined
    (C) persisted
    (D) accompanied

5. The Dorbush City Council awarded a key to the city to Ms. Mazzulo, ------- grandfather designed the city park.

    (A) what
    (B) that
    (C) who
    (D) whose

6. Lizor Consultants, Inc., has extensive experience in ------- managing corporate mergers.

    (A) slightly
    (B) commonly
    (C) successfully
    (D) originally

7. Ms. Simon's ------- to growing the company's client base earned her a bonus this year.

    (A) dedicate
    (B) dedicated
    (C) dedicates
    (D) dedication

Part 6

Questions 8-11 refer to the following advertisement.

------- for an enchanting setting for your family celebration? Why not consider the beautiful
8.
Hibiscus Tropical Garden in Tortola, British Virgin Islands? For 50 years, the site was a working
tropical flower nursery. Then fifteen years ago, the grounds and structures were completely
------- . The result of this million-dollar investment is a unique ------- of rustic charm with modern
9.   **10.**
amenities. Our converted warehouse accommodates up to 250 guests for dinner and
entertainment. When dinner is over, our state-of-the-art sound system guarantees that your
guests will be on their feet and dancing all evening long.

Our event calendar fills up quickly each season. ------- . Contact Evan Wilder at 284-555-0012 or
11.
ewilder@hibiscustropicalgarden.co.vg.

8. (A) Looked
(B) To look
(C) Looking
(D) Look

9. (A) isolated
(B) renovated
(C) abandoned
(D) rented

10. (A) combination
(B) to combine
(C) combinable
(D) combine

11. (A) Unfortunately, we no longer sell
flowering plants.
(B) The island is accessible by boat and
by plane.
(C) The best views are on the south end
of the island.
(D) So start planning your special event
today.

Section
15

GO ON TO THE NEXT PAGE ⟶

Part 7

Questions 12-14 refer to the following invitation.

CELEBRATION OF SERVICE

Come celebrate longtime employees for their dedicated service to
Astoria Industries.

Keynote address will be given by COO Henry Wilson, who will talk
about the changes he has seen in the company over the past 43 years.

*Local elected officials and all Astoria Industries
employees are welcome to attend!*

Wednesday, 10 April, 10:00 A.M. to 11:30 A.M.

A variety of light refreshments will be served.

Astoria Industries Headquarters
Conference Room B
29 Hoey Street
Kamo, Whangarei 0112

12. What is the purpose of the April 10 event?

(A) To welcome a new company executive
(B) To celebrate a company anniversary
(C) To thank a group of employees
(D) To mark the opening of a new headquarters

13. What is implied about Mr. Wilson?

(A) He is an elected official in Whangarei.
(B) He has worked at Astoria Industries for decades.
(C) He volunteered to organize the event.
(D) His office is next to Conference Room B.

14. What will most likely be served at the event?

(A) A selection of appetizers
(B) A three-course meal
(C) A lunch buffet
(D) A catered brunch

GO ON TO THE NEXT PAGE ⟶

Questions 15-19 refer to the following report, e-mail, and article.

Naro Glass, Inc.
Web Traffic Analysis
Compiled by Evan Morin

How visitors found Naro Glass, Inc.	January	February	March	April
Typed exact Web address	23,000	22,000	20,000	21,000
Used Internet search engine	19,000	20,000	21,000	18,000
Referred from client Web site	19,000	19,000	19,000	7,000*
Clicked link from social media site	17,000	16,000	14,000	13,000

*Note to follow up with Lensegent (our principal source of client referrals)

E-Mail Message

To: Evan Morin
From: Rie Kondo
Date: May 1
Subject: Web traffic

Hello Evan,

Thank you for sending me the traffic-analysis chart for our Naro Glass Web site. This is helpful. One thing that we can do to get our numbers back up is to increase our presence on sites like Zermavise. That should pull our traffic in this segment back up to the 17,000 hits that we saw at the beginning of the year. We should also broaden our list of client sites, since a problem at Lensegent seems to be dragging down our numbers in that area.

Best regards,

Rie

DENVER (May 10)—After a solid fourth quarter last year, Lensegent has had a rocky start to the new year. The company's CEO, Sara Ormond, stepped down from her post in February. Then in April, technical difficulties caused the company's Web site to crash multiple times. This month, Lensegent suspended its plan to expand overseas and announced that it would restructure its domestic sales force. All this turmoil has left investors wondering if this leader in the photographic components market can still compete. New CEO Maxwell Holland assured investors that the downturn is temporary and that his plan for restructuring Lensegent will result in a stronger company by September.

☐ **15.** Who most likely is Mr. Morin?

   (A) A salesperson
   (B) A data analyst
   (C) A company CEO
   (D) A human resources specialist

☐ **16.** When did the highest number of visitors find the Naro Glass Web site through a search engine?

   (A) In January
   (B) In February
   (C) In March
   (D) In April

☐ **17.** What most likely is Zermavise?

   (A) A Web-based newspaper
   (B) An Internet search tool
   (C) A client's Web site
   (D) A social media site

☐ **18.** What most likely caused referrals for Naro Glass from Lensegent to fall?

   (A) A change in Lensegent's leadership
   (B) A problem with Lensegent's Web site
   (C) The closure of Lensegent's international division
   (D) The restructuring of Lensegent's domestic sales force

☐ **19.** What does Lensegent make?

   (A) Camera parts
   (B) Eyeglasses
   (C) Jewelry
   (D) Computer software

Section **15**

Section

16

Part 5

1. Ms. Yi signed the checklist, certifying that she had ------- counted the boxes stored in the warehouse.

(A) arguably
(B) potentially
(C) carefully
(D) spaciously

2. During yesterday's work session Jodie Guerra took notes, ------- she will share with the group via e-mail.

(A) which
(B) them
(C) else
(D) several

3. Next month, more than 50 windows will be replaced at the ------- Northbridge Library building.

(A) amazed
(B) tentative
(C) historic
(D) residential

4. Working from home without supervisor approval is ------- prohibited.

(A) hastily
(B) tensely
(C) strictly
(D) tightly

5. The photography contest winners will have their work ------- in the library's lobby.

(A) displayed
(B) was displayed
(C) to be displayed
(D) have been displayed

6. The ------- of Vitas Gym's new swimming pool are 15 meters by 35 meters.

(A) shapes
(B) directions
(C) positions
(D) dimensions

7. Mr. Chan noted that ------- the previous quarter, his team exceeded its sales goals.

(A) while
(B) even as
(C) during
(D) nearby

Part 6

Questions 8-11 refer to the following letter.

Ainsworth HVAC: For all your home comfort needs.

Dear Valued Customer,

Our records ------- that you have an unused promotional credit for a free, no-obligation heating,
8.
ventilation, and air-conditioning (HVAC) inspection. With so many routine family and work

responsibilities on our minds, it is difficult for many people to ------- that these systems and their
9.
ductwork require proper maintenance and cleaning. ------- . However, postponing it can lead to
10.
higher energy costs and wear and tear on the ------- . Give us a call to schedule an appointment
11.
today!

Sincere regards,

Your Ainsworth HVAC Specialists

---

8. (A) show
(B) will show
(C) to show
(D) showing

9. (A) control
(B) assign
(C) remember
(D) request

10. (A) Therefore, Ainsworth HVAC thanks
you for your business.
(B) An inspection every six months can
help maintain air quality.
(C) We offer exceptional payment plans.
(D) Visit our Web site to see each of the
services we offer.

11. (A) technician
(B) process
(C) decision
(D) equipment

GO ON TO THE NEXT PAGE ⟶

Part 7

Questions 12-14 refer to the following letter.

Athena Pro Star • 575 Parkwood Street • Corvallis, OR 97330

October 14

Angelika MacGorain
214 East College Avenue
Corvallis, OR 97330

Dear Ms. MacGorain,

Thank you for purchasing an Athena Pro Star Platinum membership! Now you can take advantage of our state-of-the-art equipment, as well as our aerobics and indoor cycling classes. Also, you can use your Platinum member card for entry into any Athena Pro Star franchise location. — [1] —.

We have processed your initiation fee and prorated monthly fee, which you paid on October 9. — [2] —. From now on, you will be billed on the first of each month. — [3] —. You may make your payment in person or through our Web site. Please allow at least two days for payments made on the Web site to post to your account. — [4] —.

Sincerely,

Tamar Chivadze

Tamar Chivadze
Membership Services

---

12. What type of business is Athena Pro Star?

(A) An electronics store
(B) A fitness club
(C) A job training service
(D) A hotel chain

13. According to the letter, on what date will Ms. MacGorain next be billed?

(A) October 9
(B) October 14
(C) November 1
(D) November 3

14. In which of the positions marked [1], [2], [3], and [4] does the following sentence best belong?

"This includes any of our overseas locations."

(A) [1]
(B) [2]
(C) [3]
(D) [4]

Section

16

From:	Jon Cuthbert
To:	Farah Moosa
Date:	16 June
Subject:	Conference panel
Attachment:	📎 Possible panelists and topics

Farah,

I am putting together a panel for our upcoming Zurich Women's Leadership Conference. Participants will each give a fifteen-minute talk about their experiences in their chosen career field. Then the open panel discussion will begin.

So far, I have thought of four participants to invite, other than you. Please find the names of these potential panelists attached along with the topics that each would address. I understand that Dr. Lordachescu is a colleague of yours. If possible, could you see that the content of your talk and your contributions to the discussion are sufficiently different from hers?

By the way, could you provide me with your own suggestions for additional panelists? Get back to me soon with this, as the conference starts in mid-August, and these panel arrangements will need to be finalised by late July.

Thanks,

Jon

Proposed Topics and Panelists

Panelist	Background	Topic
Karine Bastin	Founder of national bakery chain	Women in small businesses
Cici Lordachescu	Chair of university humanities department	Women in academia
Alicia Ward	Motivational speaker	Women in freelance positions
Daniela von Theumer	Women's professional volleyball coach	Women in sports

From:	Farah Moosa
To:	Jon Cuthbert
Date:	17 June
Re:	Conference panel

Hi Jon,

Your panel plans look good. I am, however, concerned about Ms. von Theumer's topic, as I believe it does not relate closely to the others. Could she instead talk more generally about "women in the spotlight," as she and many on her team are famous?

I will get back to you shortly with one or two additional panelist suggestions. Also, could you ask each confirmed panelist to send in some biographical details so we can include these in our promotional materials?

Many thanks.

Farah

15. According to the first e-mail, when will the conference take place?

(A) In June
(B) In July
(C) In August
(D) In September

16. What is suggested about Ms. Moosa?

(A) She works at a university.
(B) She has never met Mr. Cuthbert before.
(C) She does not participate in sports.
(D) She speaks at conferences around the world.

17. According to the table, who started her own business and expanded it?

(A) Ms. Bastin
(B) Dr. Lordachescu
(C) Ms. Ward
(D) Ms. von Theumer

18. What conference panel topic is most likely to be replaced?

(A) Women in small businesses
(B) Women in academia
(C) Women in freelance positions
(D) Women in sports

19. What does Ms. Moosa request in the second e-mail?

(A) That the participants provide information about themselves
(B) That she be included in the list of panelists
(C) That Mr. Cuthbert review some promotional materials
(D) That books be made available to purchase at the conference

Section

17

Part 5

□ **1.** Vannuck gym bags are designed to ------- fit into a standard locker.

   (A) easiest
   (B) easier
   (C) easily
   (D) ease

□ **2.** The maintenance team will return tomorrow to ------- the door installation.

   (A) complete
   (B) determine
   (C) succeed
   (D) account

□ **3.** Most visitors say that their ------- feature of Jodi's Haven Inn is the private beach.

   (A) favor
   (B) favorable
   (C) favorite
   (D) favorably

□ **4.** A portion of the proceeds earned -------tonight's concert is being donated to charity.

   (A) from
   (B) of
   (C) with
   (D) up

□ **5.** Dainville Communications is ------- to double its revenue in the coming year.

   (A) expect
   (B) expected
   (C) expectantly
   (D) expectation

□ **6.** As a result of last year's renovation, the science museum's rooms were -------.

   (A) rearranged
   (B) rearranging
   (C) rearranges
   (D) rearrange

□ **7.** -------, information technology determines what and how children play.

   (A) Consecutively
   (B) Increasingly
   (C) Deeply
   (D) Highly

Part 6

Questions 8-11 refer to the following e-mail.

From: Accounts Department <accounts@binghamhomerentals.co.uk>
To: Jensen Cooper <jcooper@msqmail.co.uk>
Date: 30 April
Subject: Holiday home payment (#1452)

Thank you for renting from us the cottage at 1452 Pierce Lake for your forthcoming holiday. We are writing to inform you that your rent payment is presently two days ------- . To avoid the risk of
8.
losing your ------- , please submit your payment before close of business today. ------- .
9.   10.

We completely understand how easy it can be to simply overlook the submission of one's payment. Nevertheless, if we do not receive the payment within the next two days, we must cancel your booking and your ------- will not be refunded.
11.

Regards,

Bill Bellows
Bingham Home Rentals

□ **8.** (A) latest
(B) lateness
(C) later
(D) late

□ **9.** (A) reservation
(B) license
(C) advertisement
(D) patience

□ **10.** (A) We accept payments both through our Web site and by phone.
(B) Lake houses are available for weekly rentals from June through August.
(C) Your home may need some repairs to prepare it to rent to others.
(D) We do business with hundreds of customers every year.

□ **11.** (A) deposited
(B) depositing
(C) deposit
(D) depositor

Section
17

GO ON TO THE NEXT PAGE ———→

Part 7

Questions 12-15 refer to the following e-mail.

To:	All Barnsley Research Centre Staff
From:	Shawn Casper
Date:	3 August
Subject:	Project approved

Dear Staff:

Our request to replace the windows in the Barnsley Research Centre has been approved by corporate headquarters. The Barnsley Research Centre is more than 40 years old, making it the oldest of Solution Fibrewire's various facilities. It still has its original windows, so their replacement will give us a big boost in comfort as well as energy savings.

Contractors will complete the work during weekends, beginning with the east side of the building this Saturday. On Friday, all furniture, computers, and similar items must be removed from offices on the east side to ensure they are not damaged during the installation of the new windows. Professional movers have been contracted to carry these items to designated areas for temporary storage. We suggest that affected employees take home any personal items on Thursday and prepare to work from home on Friday. Staff who do not work on the east side of the building should report to the office as usual.

Over the following three weekends, the work will move to the west, south, and north sides of the building, respectively. If any questions arise during the process, please contact me directly.

Sincerely,

Shawn Casper
Building Manager, Barnsley Research Centre
Solution Fibrewire Ltd.

12. What is indicated about Solution Fibrewire Ltd.?

(A) Its facilities need to be expanded.

(B) It has staff in multiple locations.

(C) It was recently bought by another firm.

(D) Its head office was recently relocated.

13. What does Mr. Casper state will be the result of the completed project?

(A) Lower energy costs

(B) Quieter work spaces

(C) More efficient use of space

(D) A more modern appearance

14. What should some staff be prepared to do?

(A) Work from home

(B) Choose new offices

(C) Move their furniture

(D) Identify storage areas

15. Where will the project end?

(A) On the east side

(B) On the west side

(C) On the north side

(D) On the south side

GO ON TO THE NEXT PAGE ⟶

Questions 16-20 refer to the following e-mail, Web page, and article.

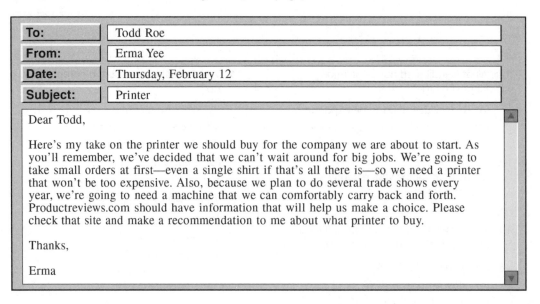

To:	Todd Roe
From:	Erma Yee
Date:	Thursday, February 12
Subject:	Printer

Dear Todd,

Here's my take on the printer we should buy for the company we are about to start. As you'll remember, we've decided that we can't wait around for big jobs. We're going to take small orders at first—even a single shirt if that's all there is—so we need a printer that won't be too expensive. Also, because we plan to do several trade shows every year, we're going to need a machine that we can comfortably carry back and forth. Productreviews.com should have information that will help us make a choice. Please check that site and make a recommendation to me about what printer to buy.

Thanks,

Erma

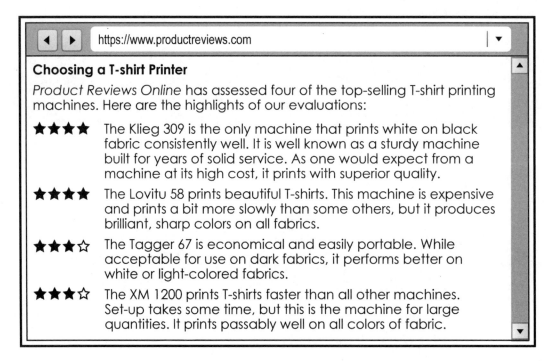

https://www.productreviews.com

Choosing a T-shirt Printer

Product Reviews Online has assessed four of the top-selling T-shirt printing machines. Here are the highlights of our evaluations:

★★★★ The Klieg 309 is the only machine that prints white on black fabric consistently well. It is well known as a sturdy machine built for years of solid service. As one would expect from a machine at its high cost, it prints with superior quality.

★★★★ The Lovitu 58 prints beautiful T-shirts. This machine is expensive and prints a bit more slowly than some others, but it produces brilliant, sharp colors on all fabrics.

★★★☆ The Tagger 67 is economical and easily portable. While acceptable for use on dark fabrics, it performs better on white or light-colored fabrics.

★★★☆ The XM 1200 prints T-shirts faster than all other machines. Set-up takes some time, but this is the machine for large quantities. It prints passably well on all colors of fabric.

Big Business in T-Shirts

By Marcus Schreiner

September 25—Those who monitor developments in the online business market will have noticed a particular trend: a boom in the number of apparel printing companies. They encourage members of the public to create and submit designs that subsequently will be printed on clothing and clothing accessories. The designs are then posted on the company's Web site, where consumers can place orders for a particular design. Designers receive a certain percentage of the profits.

Some companies, like Kimmytee, require a minimum of 100 orders before offering print services. Others, like Faymoor Clothes, work with the client to create a minimum order as low as 12 items. Still others, such as Akahi Shirts and Temizo Printing, which have been in the business for six months and ten years respectively, do not require a minimum number of orders at all.

☐ **16.** What is indicated about the Klieg 309?

(A) It is the most popular machine on the market.

(B) It has been on the market longer than its competitors.

(C) It has a reputation for being reliable.

(D) It is known for being easy to operate.

☐ **17.** What do all the machines mentioned on the Web page have in common?

(A) They print on dark fabrics.

(B) They are lightweight.

(C) They are faster than average.

(D) They are relatively inexpensive.

☐ **18.** What printer did Mr. Roe most likely recommend to Ms. Yee?

(A) The Klieg 309

(B) The Lovitu 58

(C) The Tagger 67

(D) The XM 1200

☐ **19.** In the article, in paragraph 1, line 1, the word "monitor" is closest in meaning to

(A) believe in

(B) observe

(C) supervise

(D) depend on

☐ **20.** What company mentioned in the article do Ms. Yee and Mr. Roe most likely work for?

(A) Akahi Shirts

(B) Faymoor Clothes

(C) Kimmytee

(D) Temizo Printing

Section

17

145

Section

18

Section 18 の正解数		
1回目	2回目	3回目
月　日　　　問／20問	月　日　　　問／20問	月　日　　　問／20問

Part 5

1. Since Ms. Byun's office is being painted, she will be working ------- in room 212.

(A) tightly
(B) broadly
(C) temporarily
(D) structurally

2. The employees' performance-review meetings will be ------- in the conference room.

(A) concerned
(B) told
(C) applied
(D) held

3. Ober Corporation's board of directors will meet again after the ------- of the new president.

(A) elect
(B) election
(C) elective
(D) elects

4. Job opportunities for translators are predicted to increase in the ------- ten years.

(A) next
(B) straight
(C) additional
(D) productive

5. Please silence all mobile phones once the performance ------.

(A) starts
(B) will start
(C) was starting
(D) started

6. Some of our customers prefer an aggressive approach to investment, ------- others are cautious.

(A) despite
(B) while
(C) so
(D) because

7. Author and ------- artist Jo Ng will sign copies of her latest book at the library on Monday.

(A) accomplishing
(B) accomplished
(C) accomplishment
(D) accomplish

Part 6

Questions 8-11 refer to the following notice.

Attention, All Kurlinkus Seeds Staff:

Several customers have reported issues with their orders this month. ------- , they are receiving
                8.
packets with no seeds in them. Going forward, please be sure to inspect each packet before
releasing it for distribution. We do not want to accidentally ship any more ------- packets.
                               9.
I realize that our rapid growth has put a strain on our existing operations. ------- . The
               10.
management team is currently evaluating our processes to identify how we can better meet the
growing demand while maintaining our high standards for quality. In the meantime, please be
extra diligent when ------- seeds.
       11.

Thank you!

Kurlinkus Seeds Management

---

8. (A) Therefore
   (B) Then again
   (C) Specifically
   (D) Nonetheless

9. (A) old
   (B) wet
   (C) dirty
   (D) empty

10. (A) I have received the inspection report.
    (B) You can resume work tomorrow.
    (C) They are now ready for shipment.
    (D) This issue is clear evidence of that.

11. (A) packing
    (B) a pack of
    (C) they pack
    (D) having packed

Section

18

GO ON TO THE NEXT PAGE ⟶

Part 7

Questions 12-15 refer to the following online chat discussion.

Shanice Rowe (10:12 A.M.) Good news, Minseo and Ademar. I just spoke to Mr. Perkins and he wants us to start developing a proposal for the Zeno Cement project.

Minseo Jeong (10:12 A.M.) Oh, you spoke to him already?

Shanice Rowe (10:13 A.M.) Yes, we had a brief chat. He thinks our ideas are worth pursuing. I bumped into him as he was coming out of his regular Monday morning meeting today.

Ademar Souza (10:14 A.M.) That's wonderful. So, when are we all free? I can meet after 3:00 P.M. Tuesday or Thursday this week—or anytime on Friday.

Minseo Jeong (10:15 A.M.) You're right, Ademar. We really need Mr. Perkins' support to move forward with Zeno Cement.

Shanice Rowe (10:15 A.M.) I'm free late tomorrow afternoon, or I can do Thursday at 3:30 P.M. or Friday at 2:30 P.M.

Minseo Jeong (10:16 A.M.) Can we try to meet earlier in the week? I would prefer Tuesday afternoon, if that's alright with you two.

Ademar Souza (10:17 A.M.) That's fine with me.

Shanice Rowe (10:17 A.M.) Shall we say tomorrow at 4:00 P.M.?

Minseo Jeong (10:18 A.M.) Sounds good. We can meet in the Albright Conference Room. I'll reserve it for an hour. Is that OK?

Ademar Souza (10:19 A.M.) That's great. And let's all come with rough drafts of our own so that we can combine our ideas during the meeting.

12. What is indicated about Mr. Perkins?

    (A) He specializes in cement products.

    (B) He participates in a meeting every Monday.

    (C) He has the same job as Ms. Rowe.

    (D) He is the founder of a company.

13. At 10:14 A.M., what does Mr. Souza most likely mean when he writes, "That's wonderful"?

    (A) He is surprised that the Zeno Cement project has been finalized.

    (B) He is pleased that Mr. Perkins agreed to hire more staff.

    (C) He is satisfied that a merger with Zeno Cement will proceed.

    (D) He is happy that Mr. Perkins has approved some work.

14. When will the writers gather to work together?

    (A) On Monday at 3:00 P.M.

    (B) On Tuesday at 4:00 P.M.

    (C) On Thursday at 3:30 P.M.

    (D) On Friday at 2:30 P.M.

15. What will most likely happen next?

    (A) Ms. Rowe will make a presentation.

    (B) Mr. Perkins will examine a proposal.

    (C) Ms. Jeong will reserve a room.

    (D) Mr. Souza will contact Zeno Cement.

GO ON TO THE NEXT PAGE ⟶

Questions 16-20 refer to the following Web site and announcement.

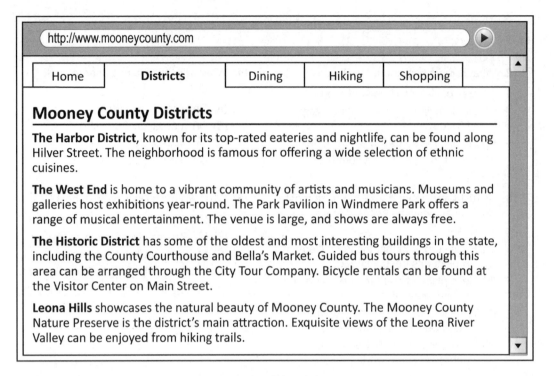

http://www.mooneycounty.com

| Home | **Districts** | Dining | Hiking | Shopping |

Mooney County Districts

The Harbor District, known for its top-rated eateries and nightlife, can be found along Hilver Street. The neighborhood is famous for offering a wide selection of ethnic cuisines.

The West End is home to a vibrant community of artists and musicians. Museums and galleries host exhibitions year-round. The Park Pavilion in Windmere Park offers a range of musical entertainment. The venue is large, and shows are always free.

The Historic District has some of the oldest and most interesting buildings in the state, including the County Courthouse and Bella's Market. Guided bus tours through this area can be arranged through the City Tour Company. Bicycle rentals can be found at the Visitor Center on Main Street.

Leona Hills showcases the natural beauty of Mooney County. The Mooney County Nature Preserve is the district's main attraction. Exquisite views of the Leona River Valley can be enjoyed from hiking trails.

Announcing: The Mooney County Parade

This popular annual event will be held next Saturday starting at noon at the County Courthouse. As usual, parade groups will march down Keel Street and turn onto Laurel Road. The route ends at Windmere Park. After the parade, the Santiago Heart band is scheduled to perform at 2:00 P.M. at the Park Pavilion. Awards recognizing the top entries in a number of categories from the parade will also be presented.

Officials are reminding citizens that vehicles will encounter detours in the vicinity of the parade route due to temporary road closures, and street parking will be very limited. Spectators are encouraged to use the shuttle bus service, which will start at 10:30 A.M. and run every 20 minutes all day.

16. For whom is the Web site most likely intended?

(A) Visitors to Mooney County
(B) Real estate developers
(C) Parade participants
(D) Government officials

17. According to the Web site, what is offered in the Harbor District?

(A) Guided bus tours
(B) A variety of dining options
(C) Scenic walking trails
(D) Notable architectural sites

18. What is NOT implied about the Historic District?

(A) It is home to a museum of history.
(B) It is suitable for riding a bicycle.
(C) A parade begins there every year.
(D) Bus tours are offered there.

19. What is indicated about the musical performance after the parade?

(A) It showcases the talents of local musicians.
(B) It is free to the public.
(C) It will be held in Leona Hills.
(D) It features an award-winning band.

20. What recommendation is made in the announcement?

(A) Avoid sections of Windmere Park that are under construction
(B) Follow Laurel Road for the best view of the parade
(C) Take public transportation to minimize traffic
(D) Arrive early in order to visit the market

Section

19

Part 5

1. All employees must remove their food from the communal refrigerator ------- leaving for the holidays.

   (A) during
   (B) onto
   (C) before
   (D) except

2. By importing items from West Africa, Asante Clothing has gained a strong position in the -------.

   (A) industry
   (B) industrial
   (C) industrialize
   (D) industrializing

3. This month Thunderbolt Foods will be ------- its production area to accommodate new equipment.

   (A) imagining
   (B) bringing
   (C) expanding
   (D) profiting

4. Fandango's sales team is developing a strategy to market the company's services more -------.

   (A) effect
   (B) effects
   (C) effective
   (D) effectively

5. Aiduk Electronics' recycling ------- will drastically decrease the amount of waste produced each month.

   (A) initiative
   (B) object
   (C) impression
   (D) preview

6. We will replace orders damaged in transit immediately ------- the product is returned.

   (A) where
   (B) beyond
   (C) after
   (D) until

7. Ensin Company distributes all its products directly to consumers ------- its competitors do not.

   (A) even though
   (B) apart from
   (C) as well as
   (D) in particular

Part 6

Questions 8-11 refer to the following press release.

The Provincial Independent Grocers Association (PIGA) announced today that Edo Dorr has been selected as the organization's president and CEO. Mr. Dorr ------- served as the organization's
8.
vice president of operations. As president, Mr. Dorr ------- on raising the public profile of
9.
independent grocers.

"------- are looking for an alternative to giant chain supermarkets," said PIGA spokeswoman
10.
Christine Franco. "The time is right for a return to convenience and personal service to lure

them back. ------- . We are confident that Edo Dorr is the right person to lead our organization
11.
forward."

☐ **8.** (A) instead
(B) likewise
(C) formerly
(D) unfortunately

☐ **9.** (A) will focus
(B) had focused
(C) was focusing
(D) could have focused

☐ **10.** (A) Farmers
(B) Promoters
(C) Shoppers
(D) Executives

☐ **11.** (A) Mr. Dorr enjoys reading in his spare time.
(B) That is exactly what PIGA grocers offer.
(C) Shopping carts should not be removed from the parking area.
(D) Prices of some staple items have decreased in recent years.

Section
19

GO ON TO THE NEXT PAGE ⟶

Part 7

Questions 12-14 refer to the following e-mail.

E-mail	
To:	Lathern Printing <rcouselo@lathernprinting.co.nz>
From:	Erin Johanson <ejohanson@jestor.co.nz>
Subject:	Print order
Date:	1 June
Attachment:	📎 The Other Party

Hello, Mr. Couselo,

I'm Erin Johanson. We just spoke together on the phone. Attached to this e-mail is the computerised picture I mentioned to you. It's of a film poster from 35 years ago. My father has directed many films in the span of his career, but *The Other Party* was the first one he ever made. We would like to have the image blown up for him as a birthday gift.

If possible, could you enlarge and print the image on a poster board that measures 69 centimetres by 104 centimetres? This would replicate the orginal dimensions. If the attached version is too small and doesn't print clearly, let me know. I will try to find a sharper image from my father's archives. Feel free to call me at 0 3634 443. Also, could you please send a cost estimate for this request before moving forward?

Thank you,

Erin Johanson

12. Who most likely is Mr. Couselo?

    (A) A former film director

    (B) A Lathern Printing technician

    (C) A friend of Ms. Johanson's

    (D) An employee of a movie company

13. What is being sent with the e-mail?

    (A) A project budget

    (B) An image of a poster

    (C) A famous document

    (D) An invitation to a party

14. What is indicated about the measurements of a poster board?

    (A) They represent the original size of an item.

    (B) They are non-standard measurements.

    (C) They will require extra expense to produce.

    (D) They are corrections to a previous communication.

GO ON TO THE NEXT PAGE ⟶

Questions 15-19 refer to the following form, e-mail, and letter.

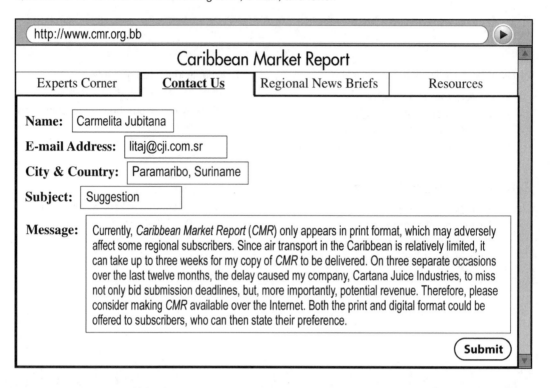

http://www.cmr.org.bb

Caribbean Market Report

| Experts Corner | **Contact Us** | Regional News Briefs | Resources |

Name: Carmelita Jubitana

E-mail Address: litaj@cji.com.sr

City & Country: Paramaribo, Suriname

Subject: Suggestion

Message: Currently, *Caribbean Market Report* (*CMR*) only appears in print format, which may adversely affect some regional subscribers. Since air transport in the Caribbean is relatively limited, it can take up to three weeks for my copy of *CMR* to be delivered. On three separate occasions over the last twelve months, the delay caused my company, Cartana Juice Industries, to miss not only bid submission deadlines, but, more importantly, potential revenue. Therefore, please consider making *CMR* available over the Internet. Both the print and digital format could be offered to subscribers, who can then state their preference.

Submit

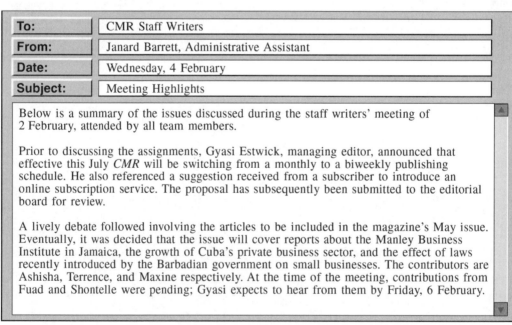

To:	CMR Staff Writers
From:	Janard Barrett, Administrative Assistant
Date:	Wednesday, 4 February
Subject:	Meeting Highlights

Below is a summary of the issues discussed during the staff writers' meeting of 2 February, attended by all team members.

Prior to discussing the assignments, Gyasi Estwick, managing editor, announced that effective this July *CMR* will be switching from a monthly to a biweekly publishing schedule. He also referenced a suggestion received from a subscriber to introduce an online subscription service. The proposal has subsequently been submitted to the editorial board for review.

A lively debate followed involving the articles to be included in the magazine's May issue. Eventually, it was decided that the issue will cover reports about the Manley Business Institute in Jamaica, the growth of Cuba's private business sector, and the effect of laws recently introduced by the Barbadian government on small businesses. The contributors are Ashisha, Terrence, and Maxine respectively. At the time of the meeting, contributions from Fuad and Shontelle were pending; Gyasi expects to hear from them by Friday, 6 February.

Caribbean Market Report
October • Vol. 5 • Number 10

Editor's Letter

Beginning with this issue, subscribers will have the option of subscribing to either the print or electronic version of the magazine (see page 10 for details). November will see the launch of *Talking Points*, a weekly show broadcast over the Internet for public access. The program will feature interviews with regional business leaders about issues and developments affecting commerce and trade in the Caribbean. And as of January of next year, both the print and digital version of *CMR* will be published every other week rather than on a monthly basis. We hope you will be pleased with these offerings.

Gyasi Estwick

---

15. What is true about Ms. Jubitana?

(A) Her products are sold only in Jamaica.

(B) Her suggestion was implemented.

(C) She will be giving an interview to *CMR*.

(D) She became a subscriber to *CMR* over a year ago.

16. Who will be discussing government regulations?

(A) Ashisha

(B) Gyasi

(C) Maxine

(D) Terrence

17. What is suggested about Fuad?

(A) He did not submit an article in time for the February 2 meeting.

(B) He joined the staff writers' team in February.

(C) He came late to a meeting.

(D) He will write an article in collaboration with Shontelle.

18. What is indicated about the *Caribbean Market Report*?

(A) The change in its publication schedule was delayed.

(B) The number of its subscribers has increased in recent years.

(C) It is funded by Cartana Juice Industries.

(D) It consists of ten pages.

19. What is mentioned about the program *Talking Points*?

(A) It will be recorded in several languages.

(B) It will be presented for the first time in November.

(C) Episodes will be broadcast on a monthly basis.

(D) Access to it is limited to *CMR* subscribers.

Section

20

Part 5

□ **1.** The Banley Hotel offers guests -------
tours throughout the surrounding region.

    (A) impressed
    (B) collected
    (C) divided
    (D) guided

□ **2.** Alika Car Sales gave Mr. Kamaka its
employee-of-the-month ------- for selling
the most cars in July.

    (A) awarded
    (B) to award
    (C) are awarding
    (D) award

□ **3.** Subline Products, Inc., boasted record
sales of its metal products this month,
despite ------- competition from local
suppliers.

    (A) intensely
    (B) intensity
    (C) most intensely
    (D) intense

□ **4.** ------- the high demand for handcrafted
furniture, Dana Custom Furnishings has
opened three new showrooms.

    (A) Now that
    (B) Provided that
    (C) Whereas
    (D) Owing to

□ **5.** Ms. Snedeker showed her ability to lead,
------- before and after her promotion to
director.

    (A) either
    (B) those
    (C) both
    (D) many

□ **6.** The proliferation of modern roadways has
helped small towns grow to sizes that
------- were inconceivable.

    (A) calmly
    (B) eagerly
    (C) finally
    (D) previously

□ **7.** Historians consulted early land maps to
determine on ------- property the oldest
tree in the county grew.

    (A) its
    (B) whose
    (C) our
    (D) their

Part 6

Questions 8-11 refer to the following article.

WELLINGTON (5 April)—Synuor Power, a leading manufacturer of wind turbine energy systems, announced today that its Z762 turbine is now fully compliant with updated industry standards. The standards were amended to ensure ------- of the country's electricity grid. The Z762,
8.
Synuor's most popular model, has been ------- to meet those standards.
9.

"With so much new technology being utilized by turbines, it was inevitable that these regulations would be changed," said Don Bok, a Synuor Power spokesperson. "We need to keep the power on. Even a temporary ------- is not acceptable. It can cause major disruptions to commerce and
10.
daily life. ------- ."
11.

☐ **8.** (A) reliability is continued
     (B) it is continually reliable
     (C) the continued reliability
     (D) continuing to be reliable

☐ **10.** (A) increase
      (B) outage
      (C) solution
      (D) process

☐ **9.** (A) modified
     (B) canceled
     (C) suspected
     (D) purchased

☐ **11.** (A) We had proposed a different set of standards.
      (B) We hope the industry will consider another course.
      (C) We have been building wind turbines for more than 30 years.
      (D) We are happy to do our part to prevent service interruptions.

Part 7

Questions 12-15 refer to the following e-mail.

E-mail

To:	Renata Lehmann; Tomas Cordeiro
From:	Stella Dupras
Date:	February 20
Subject:	Research

Hi, Renata and Tomas,

I did some initial research into firms that specialize in measuring the effectiveness of advertising. Two market-research firms stood out. I am including a quick summary below, but the three of us should meet to discuss and to plan our next steps for the rollout of the CRX3 Blender.

Industry leader Adeline Research Group (ARG) has decades of experience. ARG collects data using large-scale postal and online surveys. The quantitative focus measures how meaningful the advertising was for the target audience and how much impact the advertising had on consumer behavior.

Clarity Trend Corp (CTC) is a younger firm with a different approach. Rather than focus solely on the effectiveness of an advertisement after it has been released, CTC incorporates testing during the creative stage. It depends largely on focus groups and small-scale telephone surveys for testing at both early and late stages.

CTC's fees are slightly higher than ARG's. That said, late-stage changes increased the cost of our original CRX2 Blender campaign significantly; earlier testing could have prevented some of that expense. I would be inclined to reach out to CTC to see if this is a viable option for us.

Stella

---

12. Why did Ms. Dupras write the e-mail?

(A) To notify colleagues of a deadline
(B) To request a product development update
(C) To share information about potential contractors
(D) To describe a new advertising campaign

13. The word "quick" in paragraph 1, line 2, is closest in meaning to

(A) rapid
(B) moving
(C) bright
(D) short

14. What is suggested about CTC?

(A) It created the advertising for the CRX2.
(B) It uses the same methods as ARG.
(C) It manufactures small appliances.
(D) It was founded after ARG.

15. What will Ms. Dupras most likely do next?

(A) Negotiate a price discount
(B) Retest an existing product
(C) Obtain additional information
(D) Prepare a proposal

GO ON TO THE NEXT PAGE ⟶

From:	Alton Gilman
To:	Myeong Kwan
Date:	July 21
Subject:	Follow-up

Dear Mr. Kwan:

We spoke briefly after your session at the spring World Pipelines Conference about your company, Krestarr Group, organizing a training session for my engineering team at DQR Corporation. We had talked about two potential sessions, one on regulations for pipeline engineers regarding land use and one on the impact of pipelines on the environment. I would really like to make this happen when you are in Alberta for the fall conference.

The Krestarr Group Web site states that your company's consulting fees are $500 for sessions with up to 10 participants, $750 for sessions with up to 15 participants, $1,000 for sessions with up to 20 participants, and $1,250 for sessions with more than 20 participants. Is this information correct? I am looking forward to your prompt reply.

Sincerely,

Alton Gilman

From:	Myeong Kwan
To:	Alton Gilman
Date:	July 22
Subject:	RE: Follow-up

Dear Mr. Gilman:

I would be happy to give a session on land-use regulations to your team. My colleague, Aisha Wright, who handles environmental-impact training for our consulting firm, is also available. We will be at the conference on September 27 and 28. There's no guarantee that conference sessions would end early enough for us to give an evening workshop on those days. So it would probably be easiest for us to arrange for a session either right before or immediately after the conference.

I am available to give the training on the 26th, or Ms. Wright, who is staying in Alberta for a few days after I leave, could present her training session on the 29th. The training fees listed in your e-mail are correct. In the future you may be interested in additional seminars we offer on other topics of interest to environmental engineers, such as maintaining environmental sustainability and how to construct buildings that are energy efficient.

Please confirm which date and training session would be best for your company. I look forward to hearing from you soon.

Best,

Myeong Kwan

Training Session Schedule

Session Presenter:	Myeong Kwan
Date:	September 26
Time:	9:00 A.M.–4:30 P.M. (lunch break 12:00 P.M.–1:00 P.M.)
Location:	Keats Conference Centre Conference Room 26B
Number of Participants:	Eighteen engineers

☐ **16.** What is the purpose of the first e-mail?

(A) To confirm conference attendance
(B) To inquire about scheduling a workshop
(C) To cancel a presentation
(D) To request that a Web site be updated

☐ **17.** What is suggested about DQR Corporation?

(A) It employs hundreds of engineers.
(B) It hires outside consultants for training.
(C) It is sponsoring an international conference.
(D) It is located in Alberta.

☐ **18.** What will be the fee for Krestarr Group's training session in Alberta?

(A) $500
(B) $750
(C) $1,000
(D) $1,250

☐ **19.** In the second e-mail, the word "guarantee" in paragraph 1, line 3, is closest in meaning to

(A) permission
(B) warranty
(C) notice
(D) assurance

☐ **20.** According to the schedule, which training session was chosen?

(A) Land-use regulations
(B) Environmental impact
(C) Sustainability
(D) Energy-efficient building

公式 TOEIC® Listening & Reading トレーニング 2
リーディング編

2023 年 12 月 6 日　第 1 版第 1 刷発行

著者　　　　　ETS

編集協力　　　株式会社 エディット
　　　　　　　株式会社 群企画
　　　　　　　株式会社 WIT HOUSE

表紙デザイン　山崎 聡

発行元　　　　一般財団法人 国際ビジネスコミュニケーション協会
　　　　　　　〒 100-0014
　　　　　　　東京都千代田区永田町 2-14-2
　　　　　　　山王グランドビル
　　　　　　　電話　(03) 5521-5935

印刷・製本　　日経印刷株式会社

公式 TOEIC®
Listening & Reading
トレーニング

リーディング編

2

別 冊

正 解 ／ 訳

IIBC
一般財団法人 国際ビジネスコミュニケーション協会

公式 TOEIC®
Listening & Reading
トレーニング
リーディング編

2

別 冊

正 解 ／ 訳

一般財団法人 国際ビジネスコミュニケーション協会

ETS TOEIC®
OFFICIAL TEST
PREPARATION
AND LEARNING

目　次

Section 1　正解／訳

正解一覧

Part 5	1 (D)	2 (B)	3 (C)	4 (D)	5 (B)	6 (B)	7 (D)
Part 6	8 (B)	9 (C)	10 (D)	11 (A)			
Part 7	12 (B)	13 (D)	14 (C)	15 (B)	16 (B)	17 (D)	18 (A)

Part 5

1. 貴社の式典に当ホテルの宴会場をお選びいただき、Pugh ホテルのスタッフ一同うれしく思っております。

(A) ～を選んでいる
(B) ～を選ぶために
(C) 選ばれる
(D) ～を選んだ

2. 備品をお電話でご注文いただいた場合、翌営業日に配達されます。

(A) ～と同様に
(B) もし～ならば
(C) また
(D) どちらか一方の

3. Kyville 財団は、新たなボランティアを呼び込むための募集イベントを年に 2 回開催しています。

(A) 自発的な
(B) 自発的に
(C) ボランティア
(D) 自発的に行われた

4. Cheong さんは今週、Nustar 社在籍 20 周年を祝いました。

(A) ～を横切った
(B) ～を開発した
(C) ～を演じた
(D) ～を祝った

5. 食事はコンベンションセンターで購入してもよいですし、各種飲み物は無料で提供されます。

(A) ～を各種取りそろえること
(B) 各種取りそろえられた
(C) 各種取りそろえられたもの
(D) ～を各種取りそろえる

6. 多くの工具に事故防止用の二重安全ロックが付いておりますので、当社工具の操作ガイドをお読みください。

(A) そのようなもの
(B) 多くのもの
(C) もう 1 つのもの
(D) ～するところの

7. Joel's 海鮮料理店のオーナーは、持続可能な方法で取られた魚のみを自店で提供することにこだわっています。

(A) ～を持続させる
(B) ～を持続すること
(C) ～を持続させるために
(D) 持続可能な方法で

※Part 5、Part 6の正解以外の語句の選択肢の和訳は、多義語のものは 1 つの意味を選んで掲載しています。

Part 6

問題 8-11 は次の広告に関するものです。

Williamsen コンピューター・ソリューションズ社

お使いのパソコンの動作がいつもより遅いですか？ アプリケーションのインストールやオペレーティングシステムのアップグレードに手助けが必要ですか？ *ハードディスクをきれいにしたいですか？ 日常的なメンテナンスの問題で幾つでもお手伝いが必要でしたら、Williamsen コンピューター・ソリューションズ社にパソコンをお持ちください。当社の熟練した専門スタッフが無料で機能性のチェックを行い、最善の方策をお薦めいたします。555-0165 に今すぐお電話を。

---

*問題 9 の挿入文の訳

8. (A) 遅い
   (B) 遅く
   (C) 遅くなる［動詞の三人称単数現在形］
   (D) 遅くなっている

9. (A) 休暇の計画を立てているところですか？
   (B) もっと幅広い映画作品を利用したいですか？
   (C) ハードディスクをきれいにしたいですか？
   (D) 割引クーポンは受け取りましたか？

10. (A) ～を要求する
    (B) ～を依頼する
    (C) ～を保持する
    (D) ～を薦める

11. (A) ～を与えてください
    (B) あなたは～を与えた
    (C) ～を与えるために
    (D) あなたは～を与えるべきだったのに

Part 7

問題 12-13 は次の説明書に関するものです。

あなたのオフィスに最高の品をお選びいただきありがとうございます。箱の中には、商品番号 434837、3 層式卓上整理棚の部品が入っています。本品は壁に掛けて設置することもできますし、机の上に置くこともできます。

組み立てには、以下のものが必要です。
・マイナスドライバー
・ねじ 6 本（同梱）

まず、横木をホルダーの側面にねじで留めます。ねじを締め過ぎないようにしてください。次に、トレイを整理棚の 3 段のそれぞれに滑り込ませます。

12. この説明書はどこにあると思われますか。

    (A) ウェブサイト上

    (B) 商品の包装の中

    (C) オフィスの壁

    (D) 工具箱の中

13. 商品番号 434837 について示されていないことは
何ですか。

    (A) 2 段階の手順で組み立てることができる。

    (B) トレイが含まれている。

    (C) ねじが付属している。

    (D) 組み立てに複数人が必要である。

問題 14-18 は次の用紙と E メールに関するものです。

クライストチャーチを歩こう：Walk the World 旅行社提供の徒歩ツアー

このたびは、Walk the World 旅行社のクライストチャーチ市内ツアーにご参加いただき、ありがとうございました。当社が今後も可能な限り最高の体験を提供できますよう、少々お時間をお取りいただき、ご参加されたツアーについてお聞かせください。

お名前：Ruben Veiga　E メール：veigar@sucorreio.com.pt　ツアー日：6 月 10 日

1．ツアーで良かったことは何ですか。
景色がきれいでした、またおいしい昼食に立ち寄ったホテルは何軒かのお店に行くのに便利でした。

2．ツアーガイドの長所と短所は何でしたか。
ツアーガイドの Janine さんは幾つかの話題はよくご存じでしたが、建築については詳しくありませんでした。でも、親しみやすい人で、ツアーにふさわしい服装やツアーの所要時間を分かりやすく教えてくれました。

3．ツアーはご期待に沿いましたか。
ある程度。歩く距離と大変さは思った通りでした。ただ、散策する人全員に水を持参するよう勧めると良いのではないかと思います。

4．他に何かご意見はありますか。
ツアー前の午前 8 時 30 分の朝食は開始が遅過ぎました。午前 9 時のツアー出発までに食べるのは、ずいぶん慌ただしく感じました。

E メールメッセージ

受信者：　Ruben Veiga <veigar@sucorreio.com.pt>
送信者：　Walk the World 旅行社 <custserv@wtwt.com>
日付：　　6 月 30 日
件名：　　お客さまの最近のツアー

Veiga 様

6 月 10 日の「クライストチャーチを歩こう」ツアーにご参加いただき、誠にありがとうございました。しかしながら、期待されたような真に傑出した体験をお届けできず、申し訳ございません。参加者の方々がお食事にもっと時間を取れるよう、朝食の時間を変更いたしました。また、弊社ツアーガイドがツアーの重要な話題について知識を新たにしておくようにいたします。

Walk the World 旅行社では、お客さまのご期待に沿うよう努めておりますので、このたびの件を正したいと思います。お客さまのアカウントに 50 ドルを付与させていただきました。こちらは今後弊社のいずれのツアーにおいてもご利用可能です。弊社のツアーご参加者の 76％がリピーターのお客さまである理由をお示しできる機会を頂けますと幸いです。

敬具

Richard Levant
顧客サービス担当

---

14. 用紙の目的は何ですか。

(A) ツアーの持ち物について顧客に助言すること

(B) 新たなツアー場所の提案を募ること

(C) ツアーについての意見を入手すること

(D) 次回のツアーに参加登録すること

15. Veiga さんは Janine について何と言っていますか。

(A) 散策に出発するのが遅れた。

(B) ツアーの前に役立つアドバイスをしてくれた。

(C) パンフレットを配布しなかった。

(D) 建築様式に詳しかった。

16. Veiga さんは何を変更した方がいいと提案していますか。

(A) ルート沿いで立ち寄る場所

(B) 朝食が出される時間

(C) 選ばれるホテル

(D) 提供される食事

17. Janine さんに何が起こると思われますか。

(A) 別のツアーに異動になる。

(B) ホテルで働き始める。

(C) 朝食の割引を受ける。

(D) ツアーの内容について再研修を受ける。

18. E メールでは、Walk the World 旅行社について何が示されていますか。

(A) リピーター客が多い。

(B) 最近、新たな行き先を追加した。

(C) 2 年間営業している。

(D) クライストチャーチ散策の距離を短くした。

正解一覧

Part 5	1 (A)	2 (D)	3 (C)	4 (B)	5 (D)	6 (A)	7 (B)
Part 6	8 (A)	9 (C)	10 (B)	11 (A)			
Part 7	12 (A)	13 (B)	14 (D)	15 (C)	16 (A)	17 (D)	18 (A)

Part 5

1. Star ビジネス・アカデミーの講座に関する宣伝用資料は、日曜日の学校説明会で展示されます。

(A) 〜についての
(B) 〜の間の
(C) 〜の中へ
(D) 〜を越えた

2. Savarini 建設はこの 10 年間、地域で最大手の住宅建設会社であり続けています。

(A) 指導力
(B) 率いられた
(C) 指導者
(D) 首位の

3. Amal Alsomali さんは Zoreh 社でモバイル技術を監督する仕事を任されています。

(A) 〜を監督する
(B) 監督された
(C) 〜を監督すること
(D) 〜を監督する予定だ

4. Saiko Hinshitsu 保険では、透明性と開かれたコミュニケーションが最優先事項です。

(A) 結果
(B) 優先事項
(C) 階
(D) 名誉

5. 近々行われる Optera 化学と Clough 製薬の合併は、会議の数ある議題のうちの 1 つです。

(A) 時折の
(B) 正確な
(C) 同一の
(D) 近づいている

6. 著者は自身の小説への支援に対して、編集者たちに謝意を表明したいと考えています。

(A) 感謝
(B) 〜を感謝する
(C) 感謝の
(D) 感謝の気持ちを込めて

7. 厳しい気象状況のため、自然散策は日程が変更されます。

(A) 型通りの
(B) 厳しい
(C) 絶対の
(D) 心配そうな

Part 6

問題 8-11 は次のお知らせに関するものです。

Oaktown クラシック・シネマ（OCC）は夏の数カ月間、週末に映画チケットを半額で販売いたします。こうした夏の週末の上映映画は主に、当館が得意とするスタンダードな名作映画となる予定です。しかしながら、1 日に 1 本、通常は夕方に、最新映画も上映します。*各上映作品用のチケットのほか、マンスリーパスもご利用になれます。OCC では、映画見放題をはじめとする 3 つのオプションを提供しております。

当館は夏の上映作品リストを 5 月末までに発表する予定です。

*問題 10 の挿入文の訳

8. (A) 〜を販売する予定だ
   (B) 〜を販売した
   (C) 〜を販売していた
   (D) 〜を販売する

9. (A) 不在の
   (B) 混ざった
   (C) 最新の
   (D) 予備の

10. (A) OCC は 30 年以上にわたって営業しております。
    (B) 各上映作品用のチケットのほか、マンスリーパスもご利用になれます。
    (C) 劇場には売店がございますので、外部からの飲食物のお持ち込みはできません。
    (D) 昨年、OCC は改修のため 2 週間閉館しました。

11. (A) 〜までに
    (B) 〜に
    (C) 〜の内部に
    (D) 〜のそばに

Part 7

問題 12-13 は次のテキストメッセージのやりとりに関するものです。

Kelly Riva [午前 9 時 39 分] お疲れさま、Linda。私は今日の午後 6 時にビデオチャットで就職の面接があります。ホテルの私たちの部屋のデスクでそれをしたいんです、あそこなら十分明るいし、壁も無地なので。その時間、部屋にいますか。

Linda Molinari [午前 9 時 40 分] 私は Oakview でクライアントと夕食の予定です。6 時半までに戻ろうかと考えていましたが。その頃には面接は終わっていると思いますか。

Kelly Riva [午前 9 時 41 分] <u>1 時間くらいかかる予定です。</u>

Linda Molinari [午前 9 時 42 分] 分かりました。夕食が長引いてもクライアントはたぶん気にしないでしょう。面接、がんばってください！

Kelly Riva [午前 9 時 43 分] ありがとう！

12. Molinari さんと Riva さんについて正しいと思われることは何ですか。

   (A) ホテルで同じ部屋に宿泊している。

   (B) 新聞記者として働いている。

   (C) Oakview に住んでいる。

   (D) 2 人とも仕事を探している。

13. 午前 9 時 41 分に、Riva さんは "It will take about an hour" という発言で、何を示唆していますか。

   (A) Molinari さんと一緒に夕食をとりたい。

   (B) Molinari さんに予定よりも遅くに戻ってほしい。

   (C) Molinari さんが面接の用意ができていることを望んでいる。

   (D) Molinari さんがビデオチャットに参加できないことを残念に思っている。

問題 14-18 は次の記事と事業計画概要に関するものです。

非営利団体のための事業計画概要
Olga Sokolinsky 記

非営利団体が事業を維持するために資金を申請するのは一般的なことだ。そうした団体は、さまざまな出資者、例えば財団、企業、政府機関といったところから提供される補助金を確保するために説得力のある事業計画概要を作成する必要がある。

事業計画概要は、供与者（資金を提供する組織）がその非営利団体の使命を手早く理解するのに役立つ要約だ。供与者となり得る組織が資金提供の依頼を検討する際に、補助金申請の資料の中でもとりわけ中心的に読むものであるため、明確かつ簡潔に書かれていなけ

ればならない。

まず、自団体が何をしているのか、団体の核となる価値観は何かを説明する。次に、多くの場合、団体とその主要役員の簡単な来歴を示す。それと同時に、団体がどのように成長し、変遷してきたかといった特筆すべき事実を取り上げる。通常、全ての資金源の簡潔な財務概要も含める。

ポーク郡テクノロジー連合
事業計画概要

私たちの使命：ポーク郡テクノロジー連合は、生活向上の助けとなるように、ポーク郡住民に快適で低料金のコンピューター講習を提供する非営利団体です。

テクノロジー連合はポーク郡在住の数人の教育者グループによって 3 年前に設立されました。彼らは、同郡の成人を対象にしたコンピューター技能の補習教育の必要性に気付いたのです。こうした技能を伸ばすことは、受講生の自信を培うのに役立ち、彼らが良い就職口を見つける助けになります。初級から上級のコンピューター講習が現在、週 2 回開催されています。地元の学校が教室を無償で貸してくれています。受講生が支払うのは 12 週の学期でわずか 35 ドルで、支払いが困難な受講生は奨学金を利用できます。テクノロジー連合は現在、初年度の約 2 倍の数の受講生に講習を提供し、来年度はさらに多くの受講生を集める見込みです。当連合の講習は現在のところ、資格を有する講師 3 名によって行われていますが、間もなくさらに 1 名の講師を採用する予定です。

14. 記事は誰に向けられたものですか。

(A) ポーク郡の新しい住民

(B) 求職者

(C) 技術講師

(D) 非営利団体

15. 記事によると、事業計画概要の目的は何ですか。

(A) 政府の規制に従うこと

(B) 組織指導者の人物紹介を書くこと

(C) 資金を獲得すること

(D) 従業員候補者を引き付けること

16. テクノロジー連合の事業計画概要について正しいことは何ですか。

(A) もっと長い計画書の一部である。

(B) 以前の提出物の改訂版である。

(C) テクノロジー連合の講師によって書かれた。

(D) 締め切りのずっと前に提出された。

17. テクノロジー連合について何が示されていますか。

(A) 施設の賃借料を支払っている。

(B) 講習は 35 分間である。

(C) 在籍者数が最近減った。

(D) 各レベルで週 2 回の講習がある。

18. 事業計画概要の第 2 段落 8 行目にある "draw" に最も意味が近いのは

(A) ～を引き付ける

(B) ～の概略を述べる

(C) ～を教える

(D) ～を促進する

Section 3 正解／訳

正解一覧

Part 5	**1** (D)	**2** (C)	**3** (D)	**4** (C)	**5** (D)	**6** (D)	**7** (A)
Part 6	**8** (B)	**9** (C)	**10** (D)	**11** (A)			
Part 7	**12** (C)	**13** (C)	**14** (B)	**15** (C)	**16** (B)	**17** (C)	**18** (A)	**19** (D)

Part 5

1. Bon-hwa's 編物社は同社のハイランドスプリングス店をリッチモンドの繁華街に移転する計画を今週先立って発表しました。

(A) 〜の方へ
(B) 両方の
(C) 過ぎゆく
(D) より早い時期に

2. 市のプロジェクトに携わる請負業者は、公正な雇用慣行に関する市の規定を順守しなければなりません。

(A) 〜を提案する
(B) 〜と想定する
(C) 従う
(D) 〜を伝える

3. 地域の農家は今年の作物栽培方法に最新技術をうまく適用しています。

(A) 成功 [名詞の単数形]
(B) 成功 [名詞の複数形]
(C) 成功した
(D) うまく

4. 『グローブストリート新聞』は、訂正が判明次第、速やかにそれを掲載しております。

(A) 利益
(B) 信念
(C) 注目
(D) 要求

5. Furnikor 社の法務部門は、新規建造物が確実に全ての規定を満たすよう、常に地元当局と連絡を取り合っています。

(A) 所在地
(B) 位置を示している
(C) 〜の位置を示す
(D) 地元の

6. Samantha's サンドイッチ店は、Han さんが退職して 2 週間以内に新しい店長を見つけることができました。

(A) 〜以来
(B) 〜を除いて
(C) 〜の間中
(D) 〜以内に

7. Reanta 金融グループは従来型の融資を利用できない起業家たちに資金を提供します。

(A) 利用する機会
(B) 利用のしやすさ
(C) 利用可能な
(D) 〜を利用すること

Part 6

問題 8-11 は次の記事に関するものです。

アーティストが歩いて創造性を見い出す

アーティストでデジタルコンテンツ管理者の Stacy Aham は、自身の時間管理能力と創造面での成功はシンプルな習慣のおかげだと考えている──毎日の散歩だ。Aham さんは必ず毎日、近所を少なくとも 1 マイルは歩くことにしている。

「それはこれからの一日に備えるのに役立ちます」と Aham さんは話す。「6 カ月ほど前、ジムの会員資格と運動のクラスを解約しました。基本的に、たいていの場合車は自宅の私道に置きっ放しにすることに決めて、今はどこへでも歩いて行きます。これまでの人生で一番健康ですね。目的もなく歩き回ることによって、芸術的なアイデアも発見できるんです」と彼女は言う。「周囲の自然環境が刺激を与えてくれます。*春は特にそうですね」。

その結果、Aham さんは自分のアイデアに自信を深め、目標により集中できるようになっている。

---

*問題 10 の挿入文の訳

8. (A) 〜にした
    (B) 〜にする
    (C) 〜にするだろう
    (D) 〜にしていた

9. (A) 何でも
    (B) 何か
    (C) どこへでも
    (D) どこか他の所で

10. (A) 私はいつも必ずコートを着るようにしています。
    (B) おそらく、この状態は長くは続かないでしょう。
    (C) 来月、私は仕事に復帰するつもりです。
    (D) 春は特にそうですね。

11. (A) その結果
    (B) 即決で
    (C) 逆に
    (D) 簡潔に

Part 7

問題 12-14 は次のメモに関するものです。

メモ

宛先： Viateur ホテル職員
差出人： Fiona Donlon 総支配人
日付： 1 月 17 日
件名： 重要なお知らせ

当ホテル内の全ての電球を、よりエネルギー効率のよい電球に交換します。ホテルの保守スタッフが月曜日からこの交換作業に取りかかります。ロビーと廊下の照明設備から始めて、その後、個々の客室へ移っていきます。皆さんは、いつもの定型業務については何も変更する必要はありません。ただ、これから 1 〜 2 週間は、おそらくホテル内で普段より動きが多くなるであろうことを知っておいていただきたいと思います。

廊下に物がない状態にしておくために、皆さんができることをしてください。作業がなるべく効率よく完了できるよう、作業員の邪魔にならないようにしてください。これは、ここ Viateur ホテルのエネルギー費用を削減するために実施する幾つかの変更の 1 つです。

ご協力のほど、よろしくお願いいたします。

---

12. メモの目的は何ですか。

(A) 宿泊客向けの新たなサービスを告知すること

(B) 特別提供に関する詳細を知らせること

(C) 近々実施される作業について説明すること

(D) イベントにスタッフを招待すること

13. 第 2 段落 1 行目にある "clear" に最も意味が近い
のは

(A) 簡単な

(B) 狭い

(C) 何もない

(D) 明るい

14. ホテルにおける変更について Donlon さんは何と
言っていますか。

(A) 新たな政府の政策に対応したものである。

(B) 経費節減を目的としている。

(C) より多くの顧客を呼び込むのに役立つ。

(D) 結果として空室が少なくなる。

問題 15-19 は次の記事、予定表、E メールに関するものです。

書店が開店行事を開催

リバートン（5 月 20 日）―― Riverton 書店は 5 月 26 日の土曜日、マニトバ州の文芸家や音楽家といった顔触れをゲストに迎えて開店を祝う。

店内 1 階の読書コーナーでは、地元作家が新刊書籍を朗読し、展示されている書籍にサインをする。2 階の Cozy カフェには、来店者を楽しませるためにミュージシャンが招かれている。無料の菓子が、書店近隣の事業者である Eastside ベジタリアンレストランと Little ベーカリーより提供されることになっている。

この書店は、この地域で広範囲の調査研究を行っている歴史家 Ralph Washington と、広告業界の重役だった Paolo Arellano との事業協力によるものだ。二人は郷土史に情熱を傾け、新しい作家の育成に力を注いでいる。

Riverton 書店
5 月 26 日の予定表

午後 0 時 15 分 ～ 1 時	フォークロックの二人組 Paul and Dennis がアルバム『朝の調べ』から曲を演奏。
午後 2 時 ～ 2 時 45 分	フィクション作家 Vikram Iyer がベストセラー『アバロンの休日』を朗読。
午後 3 時 ～ 3 時 45 分	Joni Beck がアコースティックギターで癒やし系のジャズとブルースを演奏。
午後 4 時 ～ 5 時	詩人 Richard Carney が受賞詩集『愚者の仮面』を朗読。

---

*E メール *

受信者：	Vikram Iyer <vikrami22@qmail.com>
送信者：	Paolo Arellano <parellano@rivertonbookstore.ca>
日付：	5 月 30 日
件名：	ありがとうございます

こんにちは、Vikram さん。

先週末は当店の開店祝いにご参加いただき、ありがとうございました。お客さま方はあなたの朗読と講演を大いに楽しんでおられました。『リバートン・タイムズ』の次号で、大盛況だった今回のイベントについての記事をご覧ください。私の共同事業者が朗読中のあなたの自然体の素敵なスナップ写真を撮ることができましたので、そちらも記事に添えられるとよいと思っています。

6 月に次のご著書が発売された際は、またのご登壇をご検討ください。当書店はいつでもあなたを歓迎いたします。

Paolo Arellano

---

15. 記事によると、Arellano さんについて正しいことは何ですか。

(A) リバートンについての本を書いた。

(B) 幾つかの会社を所有している。

(C) 2 つ以上の職業に就いたことがある。

(D) 歴史的価値のある家に住んでいる。

16. Paul and Dennis は 5 月 26 日にどこで演奏しましたか。

(A) 読書コーナーで

(B) Cozy カフェで

(C) Eastside ベジタリアンレストランで

(D) Little ベーカリーで

17. 予定表によると、ジャズミュージシャンはいつ演奏しましたか。

(A) 午後 0 時 15 分に

(B) 午後 2 時に

(C) 午後 3 時に

(D) 午後 4 時に

18. Washington さんは開店行事で何をしたと思われますか。

(A) 作家の写真を撮った。

(B) 自身のベストセラー本を朗読した。

(C) 書店の商品にサインした。

(D) 地元の歴史家たちと会った。

19. E メールは Iyer さんについて何を示していますか。

(A) 書店に資金を投資した。

(B) イベントに遅れて到着した。

(C) 最近の講演がオンラインで聞けるようになる。

(D) 自身の新刊書籍が間もなく出版される。

Section 4　正解／訳

正解一覧

Part 5	1 (C)	2 (B)	3 (A)	4 (A)	5 (A)	6 (B)	7 (C)
Part 6	8 (A)	9 (B)	10 (C)	11 (C)			
Part 7	12 (D)	13 (A)	14 (B)	15 (C)	16 (A)	17 (D)	18 (D)

Part 5

1. 北京航空の新たに改装された座席によって、旅客はフライト終了までに、くつろいだ爽快な気分になるでしょう。

    (A) ほとんど～ない
    (B) 常に
    (C) 新たに
    (D) 最も少なく

2. Page さんが従業員ピクニックを計画するのを手伝うことに興味がある方は、本人に直接連絡してください。

    (A) 誰の
    (B)（～の）人々
    (C) ～すること
    (D) あれ

3. 丈夫な構造と魅力的なデザインのおかげで、顧客は Orbando 社のブラインドとカーテンを好んでいます。

    (A) 丈夫な
    (B) 強烈な
    (C) 強引な
    (D) 健康的な

4. チームが 4 月 15 日の発売目標を達成するつもりなら、商品画像が午後 5 時までに承認されなければなりません。

    (A) ～を達成するつもりで
    (B) ～を達成する
    (C) ～を達成した
    (D) 達成されること

5. 市の裁量資金の余剰金は、学校組織と公園委員会の間で分配されました。

    (A) 分配された
    (B) 署名された
    (C) 意味された
    (D) 置かれた

6. 録音音声の不具合はほとんど検知できませんが、大音量だと聞き取れます。

    (A) 明確に
    (B) ほとんど～ない
    (C) 最近
    (D) 以前に

7. 建物の改修が完了するまで、マーケティング部はエジンバラの支社から仕事をすることになります。

    (A) 同じように
    (B) ～が原因で
    (C) ～するまで
    (D) そうでなければ

Part 6

問題 8-11 は次の報道発表に関するものです。

シンガポール──会計財務ソフトウエアのシンガポール最大手企業である Goh 技術グローバル社は、新たな最高執行責任者（COO）として Grace Ng の任命を発表した。この任命は現在行われている事業再構築プランの一環だ。Ng 氏は、シンガポールに本社がある Ridgeco 産業社の COO をはじめ、この業界における 15 年以上の経営幹部経験を携えて Goh 技術グローバル社に来る。「当社のこれほど重要な成長期に、Ng 氏にこの職務を担ってもらえることをうれしく思います」と Goh 技術グローバル社の CEO である Alan Chiang は述べる。「*彼女の専門知識は当社が前進する助けとなるでしょう。彼女はテクノロジー企業としての当社の地位を強固なものにしてくれるでしょう」。Ng 氏は 5 月 15 日に Goh 技術グローバル社で業務を開始する。

---

*問題 10 の挿入文の訳

8. (A) 供給会社
(B) 競争相手
(C) 仲間
(D) 方法

9. (A) 驚くほどの
(B) 進行中の
(C) めったに起こらない
(D) 即時の

10. (A) 彼女は以前、そのことでよく知られていました。
(B) こうしたことは以前にもあったので、多くの従業員は驚きませんでした。
(C) 彼女の専門知識は当社が前進する助けとなるでしょう。
(D) 似たような機会が得られるようになるでしょう。

11. (A) ～を強固にしていた
(B) ～を強固にしているところだった
(C) ～を強固にするだろう
(D) ～を強固にする

Part 7

問題 12-13 は次のはがきに関するものです。

<h1 style="text-align:center;">はがき</h1>

第 20 回　毎年恒例のライラック祭り

5 月 1 日から 5 月 24 日までの Vernonville ライラック祭りにご参加ください。みずみずしい花々、お食事、お飲み物、お土産、お子さまの遊び場をご家族全員でご利用になれます。今年は新しい時間帯となりますので、ご注意ください。当祭りは、毎日午前 8 時から午後 7 時まで、晴雨にかかわらず開催されます。

人出の多い週末は、チケット売り場の行列に並ばないで済むように事前にオンラインでチケットをご購入になることをお勧めいたします。当祭りのウェブサイト www.vvlilacfestival.org にアクセスしてください。10 人以上の大人数の団体さまの場合は、事務局に 616-555-0137 までお電話の上、団体チケットの割引価格についてご相談ください。

12. 祭りについて何が示されていますか。

    (A) 2年ごとに開催される。

    (B) 週末のみ開催される。

    (C) 開催場所が移った。

    (D) 開催時間が変わった。

13. 大人数の団体について何が示唆されていますか。

    (A) 割引を受けられる。

    (B) 早めの入場ができる。

    (C) ウェブサイトで登録しなければならない。

    (D) 事前にチケットを購入しなければならない。

問題 14-18 は次の規則、表、レビューに関するものです。

Sparrow Root 果樹園

果実狩りの規則

1. 購入する意思のあるものだけをお取りください。果実は果樹園を出る際に重量によるお支払いとなります。
2. 指定された区域でのみ果実を取り、お渡しする容器にお入れください。
3. お子さまには大人の同伴が必要です。
4. 木に登ったり、木を揺らしたりしないでください。

Sparrow Root 果樹園

果実狩りの収穫期カレンダー

	6月	7月	8月	9月
イチゴ	●			
モモ		●	●	
ブルーベリー	●	●	●	
リンゴ				●

http://www.localfunactivities_marimount/reviews/sparrow_root_orchard

レビュー　★★★★☆
レビュアー：Ismael Elmon

家族と私は、初めての Sparrow Root 果樹園訪問を楽しみました。摘み取ったリンゴはとてもおいしかったです！トラクターに乗車して楽しく果樹園に向かう間、トラクターの運転手さんがリンゴ狩りの規則を説明してくれました。リンゴを入れる袋は果樹園の各並木の端に使い勝手よく置かれていました。わが家の子どもたちははしごに登って高い枝から果実を摘むのをとても気に入っていました。残念なことに、別の来園者が果実を落とそうと木を揺すっているのを見かけましたが、スタッフの方がやめさせていました。少し困ったのは、駐車場が狭くて駐車スペースを見つけるのに手間取ったことです。どちらかと言うと、それはこの果樹園が大人気な証拠ですね！

14. 規則は Sparrow Root 果樹園について何を示していますか。

(A) 同園は来園者に果実を試食するように勧めている。

(B) 同園は果実の代金を重量で請求する。

(C) 同園は子ども向けのプログラムを提供している。

(D) 同園は来園者に再利用可能な容器の持参を求めている。

15. Sparrow Root 果樹園では、どの果実が最も収穫期が長いですか。

(A) イチゴ

(B) モモ

(C) ブルーベリー

(D) リンゴ

16. レビューはトラクターの運転手について何と述べていますか。

(A) 来園者に果樹園の規則を教えた。

(B) Elmon さんが駐車するのを手伝った。

(C) 最も良い果実を選ぶコツを教えた。

(D) はしごに登って Elmon さんを手伝った。

17. Elmon さんは、来園者がどの規則を破るのを見ましたか。

(A) 規則 1

(B) 規則 2

(C) 規則 3

(D) 規則 4

18. Elmon さんはいつ果樹園を訪れましたか。

(A) 6 月

(B) 7 月

(C) 8 月

(D) 9 月

Section 5　正解／訳

正解一覧

Part 5	1 (B)	2 (D)	3 (A)	4 (C)	5 (B)	6 (B)	7 (A)		
Part 6	8 (A)	9 (C)	10 (D)	11 (A)					
Part 7	12 (C)	13 (D)	14 (A)	15 (B)	16 (A)	17 (D)	18 (A)	19 (C)	20 (B)

Part 5

1. Ted Drabik は、瞬く間に電子機器部門の最も優秀な販売員になりました。

   (A) 速い
   (B) 速く
   (C) より速い
   (D) 迅速さ

2. 住宅を改築する際は、想定外の出費を予算に組み込むようにしてください。

   (A) 今なお
   (B) どちらも〜ない
   (C) あの
   (D) 〜するとき

3. 幾つかの要因が、当ウェブサイトの動画ストリーミング配信の品質に影響を及ぼす可能性があります。

   (A) 〜に影響を及ぼす
   (B) 〜に影響を及ぼすために
   (C) 影響される
   (D) 〜に影響を及ぼすこと

4. ひとたび買い物客が入店したら、出迎え係が丁重に手伝いを申し出るべきです。

   (A) 接近して
   (B) 非常に
   (C) 丁寧に
   (D) 最近

5. Suh さんは昨日は仕事に対応できなかったので、Dodd さんが彼女の代わりをしました。

   (A) 彼女自身の
   (B) 彼女を
   (C) 彼女は
   (D) 彼女自身

6. Rodrigues さんは、『週刊アクンバ』の記事が農場の温室プロジェクトに歓迎すべき注目をもたらすだろうと考えています。

   (A) 〜を公表する
   (B) 世間の注目
   (C) 広報担当者
   (D) 公表された

7. Seahurst ビルは、1 分もかからずに透明から不透明に変化する電気制御の窓ガラスを特徴としています。

   (A) 〜から
   (B) 〜に反して
   (C) 〜の間に
   (D) 〜の至る所に

Part 6

問題 8-11 は次のお知らせに関するものです。

Barrowhill 村立図書館は 8 月の間、閉館となります。数十年間にわたる地域社会への奉仕を経て、村は当館を改装する時期だと判断いたしました。改修には 2 つの段階があります。まず、館内ロビーに新しい窓を設置することから始めます。*それから、図書館全体を塗り替えます。

7 月最後の 2 週間に本を借りる方は、建物の工事が完了するまで本を借りたままで構いません。すなわち、それらの本の返却期限は 9 月 1 日となります。

*問題 10 の挿入文の訳

8. (A) ～に奉仕すること
    (B) ～に奉仕した
    (C) ～に奉仕するため
    (D) ～に奉仕していた

9. (A) 討論
    (B) コンテスト
    (C) 改修
    (D) 調査

10. (A) 図書館にはマルチメディア室もあります。
    (B) それどころか、当館はもっと図書館スタッフを雇います。
    (C) 図書館は村立博物館に隣接しています。
    (D) それから、図書館全体を塗り替えます。

11. (A) ～まで
    (B) ～の周りに
    (C) ～する所に
    (D) ～するところの

Part 7

問題 12-15 は次のテキストメッセージのやりとりに関するものです。

Liza Cho [午後 1 時 16 分] 皆さん、お疲れさまです。Emily Doley が月曜日から Josh のチームで働き始めることを改めてお知らせしておきたいと思いました。彼女は社員証を受け取るために保安課に予約を入れていますか。

Justin Bezuti [午後 1 時 20 分] オンライン上のリストには名前が見当たりません。彼女はまだ予定に入っていないようです。

Liza Cho [午後 1 時22 分] 彼女の予約が確実に新人説明会の前の朝一番になるようにしてもらえますか。

Justin Bezuti [午後 1 時 24 分] もちろん。今から保安課に電話します。

Josh Hyuk [午後 1 時 27 分] 彼女は 10 時に新人説明会に出席して、11 時頃に技術者が彼女の作業スペースのセットアップを手伝う予定です。昼食の後、彼女にはそれぞれの部署長と顔合わせしてもらおうと思っています。それは午後いっぱいかかるはずです。

Chun-Wei Kang [午後 1 時28 分] 私も彼女と給与について話をしなければなりません。理想としては、そういうことは初日に行う方がいいのですが、必要なら、火曜日の朝に延ばしても構いません。

Liza Cho [午後 1 時29分] ご対応に感謝します。彼女にはまだ記入すべき人事関係の書類が残っており、また彼女から従業員手当について質問があったときのために、私は新入社員の手引を彼女と一緒に見直したいと思っています。11 時 45 分頃、昼休みの少し前にそれをすることができるでしょう。

Justin Bezuti [午後 1 時 29 分] 分かりました。彼女の予定をまとめて、確認のために今日後ほど回覧します。

12. Doley さんは月曜日にまず何をすると思われますか。

    (A) 新人説明会に参加する

    (B) 従業員手当について聞く

    (C) 保安課に行く

    (D) 自分の作業スペースをセットアップする

13. Doley さんはいつ部署長たちとの顔合わせを始めると思われますか。

    (A) 午前 10 時

    (B) 午前 11 時

    (C) 正午

    (D) 午後 1 時

14. 午後 1 時 29 分に、Cho さんはなぜ "Thanks for accommodating" と書いていますか。

    (A) Kang さんが面談日時を変更してくれるから。

    (B) Bezuti さんが Doley さんに連絡をするから。

    (C) Hyuk さんがスケジュールを書き直したから。

    (D) Doley さんの書類が処理されたから。

15. 誰が Doley さんの月曜日の予定を配布しますか。

    (A) Cho さん

    (B) Bezuti さん

    (C) Hyuk さん

    (D) Kang さん

問題 16-20 は次の E メールと請求書に関するものです。

E メール

送信者：	Amrita Patnaik <a.patnaik@godavaririverinn.in>
受信者：	Raj Doshi <raj.doshi@delhimail.in>
送信日時：	7 月 14 日　火曜日　午前 6 時 23 分
件名：	部屋のご予約

Doshi 様

Godavari 川旅館にこの度もご宿泊予約をいただき、ありがとうございます。このメッセージは、8 月 4 日と 5 日のお部屋のご予約を確認するためのものです。当館のオンラインカレンダーにご予約を追加いたしました。本日後ほど、ご予約を確定するためにお客さまのクレジットカード番号を伺うお電話をさせていただきます。お支払い手続きはご滞在終了時まで行われませんので、ご安心ください。

ご要望に応じて、会議室 B も予約いたしました。20 名様分のお席、視聴覚機器、ティーセットを用意させていただきます。会議用にその他のご要望がございましたら、お知らせください。もし何か技術的な問題に遭遇された場合は、私が<u>解決する</u>お手伝いをさせていただきます。

またお会いできることを楽しみにしております。

敬具

Amrita Patnaik　旅館経営者

Godavari 川旅館・ナーシク市 Trimbake 通り・マハラシュトラ州　422007

お客さま情報	Raj Doshi	部屋番号	105
	Main Market、T 298 番地	宿泊料	1 泊 500 ルピー
	デリー	ご到着	8 月 3 日
	110055	ご出発	8 月 7 日

日付	明細	料金	精算
8 月 3 〜 7 日	部屋代	500 ルピー	2,000 ルピー
8 月 4 日	ルームサービス	150 ルピー	150 ルピー
8 月 5 日	会議室 B	600 ルピー	600 ルピー
8 月 5 日	ティーセット	200 ルピー	200 ルピー
8 月 5 日	ルームサービス	150 ルピー	150 ルピー
8 月 6 日	Godavari 川旅館レストラン	200 ルピー	200 ルピー
	（コンチネンタル・ブレックファスト）		
			合計：3,300 ルピー

16. Patnaik さんは 7 月 14 日に何をしたと思われますか。

(A) Doshi さんに電話をかけた。

(B) Doshi さんのクレジットカードに代金を請求した。

(C) ティーセットの準備をした。

(D) 視聴覚機器を購入した。

17. E メールの第 2 段落 3 行目にある "work out" に最も意味が近いのは

(A) 〜を行使する

(B) 〜を完成させる

(C) 〜と決定する

(D) 〜を解決する

18. Godavari 川旅館での Doshi さんの滞在について何が示唆されていますか。

(A) 当初の予定よりも長くなった。

(B) 彼がその旅館を訪れるのは初めてだった。

(C) 彼の助手によって手配された。

(D) 彼が予期していたよりも安価だった。

19. Doshi さんはいつ会議に出席したと思われますか。

(A) 8 月 3 日

(B) 8 月 4 日

(C) 8 月 5 日

(D) 8 月 6 日

20. Godavari 川旅館について何が示されていますか。

(A) 会議室は離れた場所にある。

(B) 館内にレストランがある。

(C) デリーにある。

(D) リピーターの客に割引を提供している。

正解一覧

Part 5	1 (C)	2 (C)	3 (D)	4 (D)	5 (B)	6 (C)	7 (D)
Part 6	8 (D)	9 (B)	10 (A)	11 (B)			
Part 7	12 (D)	13 (B)	14 (B)	15 (D)	16 (A)	17 (C)	18 (C)

Part 5

1. 検査官は、図書館は今後 5 年以内に新しい屋根が必要になると指摘しました。

(A) 〜について
(B) 〜の下に
(C) 〜以内に
(D) 〜より上に

2. Veloque 社は、自社のソーシャルメディアコンテンツを管理するコミュニケーション専門家を採用しました。

(A) 〜を予期する
(B) 〜を占める
(C) 〜を管理する
(D) 〜を発音する

3. 地元の起業家のための資源提供元一覧が、最近『バーガンズ・ビジネスジャーナル』に掲載されました。

(A) 臨機応変に
(B) 機転の利く
(C) 資源提供を受けた
(D) 資源

4. Jespersen 仕立屋では、正確なサイズ測定を確実にするため採寸が 2 回行われます。

(A) 効率的な
(B) 起こりそうな
(C) 注目に値する
(D) 正確な

5. McLane-Winn 社は、30 カ所以上に営業所を持つ繊維製品の大手卸売業者です。

(A) 状況
(B) 場所
(C) 関係先
(D) 職業

6. 上手な書き手はしばしば、読み手の興味を維持するために文の構造に変化を付けます。

(A) 変化を付けられた
(B) 〜に変化を付けること
(C) 〜に変化を付ける
(D) 変化を付けられるために

7. Octipro 社の最高経営責任者 Leora Han は、退職する従業員の一人一人に特別な贈り物をしました。

(A) 〜するものは何でも
(B) 私たちのもの
(C) これ
(D) それぞれ

Part 6

問題 8-11 は次の招待状に関するものです。

San Pedro 写真芸術家協会は、7 月 21 日から 7 月 24 日まで Rio Bayas 会議場で開催される毎年恒例の勉強会に皆さんをご招待いたします。このイベントは毎年、真摯な写真家の皆さんが静かで眺めのいい場所に集い、互いの作品を共有する機会となっています。今年は、プログラムが午前と午後両方のセッションに拡大されます。参加者の皆さんは、各セッションで紹介する作品のプリントまたはデジタルファイルを数枚ご持参ください。勉強会の費用は 800 ドルで、部屋代、食事代、チップが含まれています。*非会員の方は別途プログラム会費 25 ドルをお支払いください。

*問題 11 の挿入文の訳

8. (A) 最初の
(B) 毎月の
(C) 早い
(D) 年 1 回の

9. (A) 彼らは
(B) 彼らの
(C) 彼らを
(D) 彼ら自身

10. (A) 参加者
(B) 主催者
(C) 候補者
(D) 監督者

11. (A) 同会議場は多くの展示会を主催しています。
(B) 非会員の方は別途プログラム会費 25 ドルをお支払いください。
(C) 協会では写真投稿のご要望を E メールでのみ受け付けております。
(D) 当方の会員の大半は軽量のデジタルカメラを使用する方を好みます。

Part 7

問題 12-13 は次の案内板に関するものです。

WESTOVER ビル
入居者表示板

Phi 輸入サービス社 ……………	100 号室	Rivera & Pao 法律事務所 ………	200 号室
Starcrest 保険会社 ……………	145 号室	Cormac 広告社 …………………	255 号室
Callon Hill 融資社 …………	180 号室	Burchell 投資グループ …………	275 号室

賃貸・保守管理　Kellan ホールディングス社　555-0198

---

12. この案内板はどこに掲示されていると思われますか。

    (A) ホテルの受付

    (B) ショッピングモール

    (C) 法律事務所

    (D) ビルのロビー

13. Kellan ホールディングス社はどんな業務をおそらく行っていますか。

    (A) 職業相談

    (B) 不動産管理

    (C) 企業投資

    (D) 建築設計

問題 14-18 は次の E メールと提案書に関するものです。

受信者：	Rebecca Hogan <rhogan@aldfairmarket.com>
送信者：	Alex Griffith <agriffith@swynhaminternational.com>
日付：	4 月 16 日
件名：	Aldfair マーケット社様への提案書
添付ファイル：	🔗 提案書

Hogan 様

Swynham インターナショナル社による Aldfair マーケット社様のための新しい冷暖房設備の提案書を添付いたします。御社の事業規模と拡張計画に関する先週火曜日のお電話での協議に基づき、3 トン、11 万 BTU の設備を推奨いたします。このサイズであれば、御社で計画されている店舗拡張まで、今後 4 ～ 6 年間は冷暖房のご要望を十分に満たせるはずです。

提案書には、本体価格および消費税と送料を含めた総額が記載されています。当社では、現在の送料（今月のみ有効）に基づいて、この大変お得な価格をご提示することができます。この価格で確定するには、14 日以内にお電話または E メールにてご了承の旨をお知らせください。なお、ご希望であれば、御社の地域にございます弊社提携企業 Kermec 社による設置も別途低費用にて承れますことをお知らせいたします。

ご不明な点がございましたら、ご連絡ください。

敬具

Alex Griffith
Swynham インターナショナル冷暖房社　営業部長

Swynham インターナショナル冷暖房社

East Hartwick 通り 14782 番地、デトロイト、MI 48205

提案書の日付：4 月 16 日
提出先：Aldfair マーケット社様　Bartlett 通り 561 番地、アルピナ、MI 49707
宛名：Rebecca Hogan 様

推奨設備：3 トン、11 万 BTU ガス暖房／電気冷却屋上設備
　　　　　（本設備は 10 年間の製造元保証付きです）
型番：BVOHTF77592

本体価格：	3,700 ドル
消費税（6%）：	222 ドル
送料：	175 ドル
合計金額：	4,097 ドル

現地提携企業による設置を 350 ドルでご利用いただけます。

14. Griffith さんは電話で Hogan さんと何について話し合ったと思われますか。

(A) Swynham インターナショナル社の 4 年間の販売計画

(B) Aldfair マーケット社の冷暖房のニーズ

(C) Hogan さんの 5 月のデトロイト訪問計画

(D) Aldfair マーケット社までの車での道順

15. なぜ E メールで示された見積もりは 14 日間のみ有効なのですか。

(A) 2 週間以上先の設置は予定を組めない。

(B) 翌月に消費税が上がる。

(C) 商品保証が切れる。

(D) 送料が上がる可能性がある。

16. 提案書は、推奨設備について何を示していますか。

(A) 建物の屋上に設置されるように設計されている。

(B) 価格が大幅に割り引かれている。

(C) 届くまで 2 週間かかる。

(D) 2 つに分けた梱包で配送される。

17. 推奨設備は製造元によって何年間保証されていますか。

(A) 4

(B) 6

(C) 10

(D) 14

18. Kermec 社による作業には幾らかかりますか。

(A) 175 ドル

(B) 222 ドル

(C) 350 ドル

(D) 4,097 ドル

Section 7　正解／訳

正解一覧

Part 5	**1** (D)	**2** (D)	**3** (A)	**4** (A)	**5** (D)	**6** (C)	**7** (B)
Part 6	**8** (B)	**9** (C)	**10** (C)	**11** (D)			
Part 7	**12** (A)	**13** (D)	**14** (B)	**15** (C)	**16** (D)	**17** (A)	**18** (D)

Part 5

1. 全ての助成金申請書は、委員会の綿密な審査を受けなければなりません。

(A) 〜を検査する
(B) 〜を移す
(C) 〜を見積もる
(D) 〜を受ける

2. 四半期会議でプレゼンをしたい方はどなたも、Jamak さんに連絡しなければなりません。

(A) 〜を望んでいた
(B) 〜を望んだ
(C) 〜を望むだろう
(D) 〜を望んでいる

3. Sousa さんは、誤った電気配線が故障の原因だと発見しました。

(A) 欠陥のある
(B) 忍耐強い
(C) 十分な
(D) 不安な

4. 経理部が作成した監査結果は期限どおりで正確でした。

(A) 正確な
(B) 精度
(C) 正確さ
(D) 正確に

5. Ruth Ann Beachell は才能あふれる木工職人で、その作品は洗練されたデザインと飾らない実用性で知られています。

(A) 〜のように
(B) どのように
(C) ほとんどの
(D) その人の〜

6. Krogh 建築博物館の入場料には、図版が魅力的に掲載されたカタログが含まれています。

(A) 魅力
(B) 引き付けるもの
(C) 魅力的に
(D) 引き付けられた

7. この 1 年間、Ott 教授は Oaktown の歴史について広範囲にわたる研究を行ってきました。

(A) 臨時の
(B) 広範囲の
(C) 人工の
(D) 即時の

Part 6

問題 8-11 は次の記事に関するものです。

クレイグスボロー（7月21日）——かつてのゴルフ場を地域の憩いの場に転用する5年間のプロジェクトを経て、Gildermere 公園が7月26日（土）に一般に開放される。新しい公園には、約25キロメートルのウォーキングとサイクリングのコース、さらに2つの小さな植物園がある。*植物園のうちの1つは、この地域原産の花々が目玉となる予定だ。

クレイグスボロー郡の首長 Steven Ramanithy 氏が郡の職員ならびに地元住民とともに開園式に出席する予定である。全体で、この式典には400人以上が集まる可能性がある。首長は、この公園の開発を積極的に支持してきたが、この公園によってより多くの地域住民が新鮮な空気と運動を定期的に楽しめるようになると指摘する。加えて、この公園は地元での環境保護の取り組みにおける意義深い一歩だとして地域社会の指導者たちから歓迎されている。

---

*問題8の挿入文の訳

8. (A) 一部の公園利用者はずっと自分の自転車に鍵をかけていなかった。
   (B) 植物園のうちの1つは、この地域原産の花々が目玉となる予定だ。
   (C) その代わりに、10キロメートルの一本道が再舗装される予定である。
   (D) これらは開園日に来園者に配布される予定である。

9. (A) 比較すると
   (B) 以前に
   (C) 全体で
   (D) 例えば

10. (A) 彼の
    (B) どちらか一方の
    (C) その人は〜
    (D) もう1人の

11. (A) 意義深く
    (B) 意義
    (C) 〜を意味する
    (D) 意義深い

Part 7

問題 12-13 は次の E メールに関するものです。

受信者：	研究開発部職員
送信者：	Laurel Altmann
日付：	7 月 10 日
件名：	Decker 博士

職員各位

Marabay 研究所での 15 年間の勤務を終え、上級科学研究員 Rosamond Decker は、ニュージーランドに移って Wareham 大学工学部教授陣に加わるために退職します。Decker 博士の送別会は 7 月 24 日午後 7 時より Bistro Georgiana にて開催されます。Marabay での博士の業績をたたえるとともに、彼女の情熱の 1 つである教職への復帰に際し、幸運を祈ってプレゼントを贈る予定です。

参加の意向をお知らせいただくには、こちらで参加見込人数を把握できるように www.marabaylabs.com/events/4591 でご登録ください。プレゼント用の寄付をされたい場合は、内線 256 の Jake Woloch までご連絡ください。

よろしくお願いいたします。

Laurel Altmann　事務長
研究開発部

12. なぜ Altmann さんは E メールを送りましたか。

    (A) 従業員を祝賀会に誘うため

    (B) 新たに雇用された科学研究員を紹介するため

    (C) 受賞者を発表するため

    (D) ある職員の昇進について従業員に通知するため

13. Decker 博士について何が示唆されていますか。

    (A) もともとニュージーランド出身である。

    (B) Marabay 研究所に寄付をした。

    (C) Woloch さんの指導に当たっている。

    (D) 教職を受諾した。

Section
7

問題 14-18 は次のガイドラインと 2 通の E メールに関するものです。

カムハースト・ヘラルド紙
読者投稿に関するガイドライン

カムハーストのタウン紙として、地元読者のさまざまな視点を紹介する寄稿コラムならびにお便りを歓迎します。Carl Shen まで、c_shen@camhurstherald.com にそれらをお送りください。投稿の締め切りは月曜日です。週刊版は毎週金曜日に有料会員に郵送されます。

・寄稿コラムは 500 語までの長さが上限で、どんな題材に関するものでも構いませんが、地元の関心事を優先します。執筆者はプロフィール写真をご提供いただく必要があります。

・編集者へのお便りは 300 語以内とし、地元の問題を扱ったものでなければなりません。

投稿されるコラムやお便りはいずれも合理的かつ事実に基づいた議論を提示し、礼節を保って意見を表明するものでなければなりません。報道発表や陳情は掲載いたしません。

スペースの制約上、受領した全ての投稿を紙面に掲載することはできませんが、全投稿をオンラインで www.camhurstherald.com/opinion にてご覧になれます。

受信者：	c_shen@camhurstherald.com
送信者：	mona.herrera@cranmail.net
日付：	4 月 1 日
件名：	読者投稿
添付ファイル：	📎 土地区画、M.Herrera_ 写真

Shen 様

3 月 29 日の『カムハースト・ヘラルド』に、現在町議会で検討中の新しい土地区画規制に関する論説が掲載されました。新しいフランチャイズ店オーナーとして、私はこの話題をずっと注意深く見守ってきました。執筆者がこの規制が商業地区で小売業を始める妨げになると主張しているのは誤解だと思います。添付の意見を所定の写真と共に提出いたします。

よろしくお願いいたします。

Mona Herrera

受信者：	mona.herrera@cranmail.net
送信者：	c_shen@camhurstherald.com
日付：	4 月 9 日
件名：	Re: 読者投稿

Herrera 様

先週号について、私に追ってボイスメールのメッセージを頂き、ありがとうございます。固定資産税増税のニュースが、読者投稿をはじめ、他の全てを脇に追いやってしまいました。あなたのご投稿は当紙の基準を満たしておりますので、次週発行の号に掲載される予定です。お待たせして申し訳ありません。

よろしくお願いいたします。

Carl Shen

14. ガイドラインは『カムハースト・ヘラルド』について何を示唆していますか。

   (A) カムハーストの住民に無料で郵送される。

   (B) 主に町の出来事に重点を置いている。

   (C) 地元企業の一覧を保持している。

   (D) 同紙ウェブサイトのデザインを変更した。

15. Herrera さんは『カムハースト・ヘラルド』に何を投稿しましたか。

   (A) 陳情

   (B) 報道発表

   (C) 寄稿コラム

   (D) 編集者へのお便り

16. 同紙の 3 月 29 日の記事はどの話題について論じましたか。

   (A) 商業地区の新たな交通パターン

   (B) 小売店舗数の増加

   (C) 地方自治体の選挙

   (D) 新しい土地区画規制案

17. Herrera さんの投稿について何が示唆されていますか。

   (A) 理にかなった視点を示している。

   (B) 上限の長さを超えている。

   (C) オンライン上でのみ掲載される。

   (D) 間違った相手に送られた。

18. なぜ Shen さんは Herrera さんに E メールを出しましたか。

   (A) 誤りを訂正するよう頼むため

   (B) 『カムハースト・ヘラルド』紙を定期購読するよう頼むため

   (C) 常勤の記者になるよう勧めるため

   (D) 彼女の投稿の掲載が遅れていることを説明するため

正解一覧

Part 5	1 (B)	2 (A)	3 (B)	4 (C)	5 (C)	6 (C)	7 (A)	
Part 6	8 (B)	9 (C)	10 (A)	11 (B)				
Part 7	12 (C)	13 (B)	14 (C)	15 (C)	16 (C)	17 (A)	18 (A)	19 (C)

Part 5

1. 乗客は通常、列車に乗る前に切符を提示すること
を求められます。

(A) 〜よりもむしろ
(B) 通常は
(C) 〜の間で
(D) 〜でなければならない

2. 1月には、ロビー内にレストランが開店し、おい
しいお食事と魅力的な雰囲気をご提供します。

(A) 魅力的な
(B) 魅力的に
(C) 魅力的な人
(D) 魅力

3 採用担当者は、初級編集者職への応募者数が少な
かったことで当然ながら落胆しています。

(A) もっともな
(B) 当然ながら
(C) 正当化している
(D) 正当化できる

4. そのショッピングセンターの設計の大きな欠点
は，十分な駐車スペースがないことでした。

(A) 部門
(B) 部分
(C) 欠点
(D) 責任

5. Ito 博士は、昨日技術者たちによって提案された
ものよりもコストのかからない保存技術を探究す
る予定です。

(A) 十分な量
(B) それ自体
(C) それら
(D) より少ないもの

6. 寄付者たちが寄付の約束額を大幅に増やして初め
て、市民歯科診療所は目標を達成できるでしょう。

(A) 〜の場合に
(B) 〜でさえ
(C) 〜の場合に限って
(D) 〜を除いて

7. 対象市場が異なるため、地域の販売代理店は社内
営業部門とは独立して仕事をします。

(A) 独立して
(B) 熱心に
(C) 熟練して
(D) 首尾よく

Part 6

問題 8-11 は次の手紙に関するものです。

---

1 月 5 日

従業員各位

Daville 社取締役会を代表して、GPD 石油・ガス社の買収をお知らせできることを誇りに思います。*Daville社は
いまや、地域最大手の石油・天然ガス販売会社です。両社の合併は、管理部門が合理化されるに伴い、10 億ドル
を超えるコスト削減につながると見込まれています。

この合併がもたらす 1 つの大きな変更は、メルボルン近郊の Baker 製油所の閉鎖です。同製油所に現在配属され
ている全従業員は他の施設に異動となります。それに加え、当社のニュージーランドとアラブ首長国連邦の既存
施設において精製が増やされる予定です。詳細は近日中にお知らせします。このたびの素晴らしい機会をもたら
してくれた皆さんの多大な努力に私たちが感謝しておりますことをお伝えしたいと思います。

敬具

Johnson B. Falworth
取締役会事務局長
Daville 社

---

*問題 8 の挿入文の訳

8. (A) GPD 石油・ガス社は最近、創立 40 周年を祝
いました。
   (B) Daville 社はいまや、地域最大手の石油・天
然ガス販売会社です。
   (C) 当社への投資にご関心をお持ちいただき、あ
りがとうございます。
   (D) 新たな取締役会が 3 年ごとに選出されます。

9. (A) 〜を予想する
   (B) 〜を予想している
   (C) 予想されている
   (D) 〜をずっと予想している

10. (A) 閉鎖
    (B) 購入
    (C) 献身
    (D) 建設

11. (A) 実際には
    (B) 加えて
    (C) 〜の場合に
    (D) ある意味では

Part 7

問題 12-14 は次の記事に関するものです。

銀行と法曹界が
Stiedemann's を後押し

ロンドン（4 月 22 日）── Stiedemann's にとって、創業 1 年目はとても良い年となった。昨年 4 月に Rye 通りにオープンして以来、200 万ポンド近い売り上げがあったとこの家具小売店は発表している。

この成功の多くは、近隣の銀行や法律事務所によるオフィス用机と椅子の大量購入がけん引している。Stiedemann's の所有者 Michaelina Lin によると、オフィス用品が同店の売り上げの半分を占めたが、これは業界では異例のことだ。*通常、そういった商品が占めるのは全売り上げの 4 分の 1 である。

Lin 氏は、この売り上げは今後 6 カ月で減速すると予想する。というのも、オフィスの机の買い換えは 5 年以上経てからになる傾向があるためだ。こうした理由から、Stiedemann's は今後 2 年間は家庭用家具の全商品を精力的に宣伝していく予定だ。

「当社は居住者のお客さまを引き付ける取り組みを引き続き拡大していきます」と Lin 氏は語った。

*問題 14 の挿入文の訳

12. Stiedemann's はどんな種類の事業ですか。

(A) 銀行

(B) 法律事務所

(C) 家具店

(D) 不動産仲介業者

13. Stiedemann's は事業を始めてどのくらい経ちますか。

(A) 6 カ月

(B) 1 年

(C) 2 年

(D) 5 年

14. [1]、[2]、[3]、[4] と記載された箇所のうち、次の文が入るのに最もふさわしいのはどれですか。

「通常、そういった商品が占めるのは全売り上げの 4 分の 1 である」

(A) [1]

(B) [2]

(C) [3]

(D) [4]

問題 15-19 は次の広告、フォーム、E メールに関するものです。

販売業者様：バルバドス国際見本市の スペースのご予約を！

9 月 14 〜 15 日 (土曜日〜日曜日)　　　　　　　　　　　　**Bridgetown 協議会場**

バルバドス国際見本市が、幾つかの注目に値する変更点を伴って、今年も開催されます。当見本市は 2 日目を追加し、販売業者様により広いスペースをご提供できる新たな会場に場所を移します。さらに、展示場所の割り当てを受けるのではなく、今回は販売業者様がご希望の展示ブースをお選びになれます。7 月 1 日までに予約してくださった販売業者様は、25 パーセントの割引を受けられます。今すぐスペースをご予約ください！

バルバドス国際見本市は、地元で仕入れられ、生産された製品のための、この地域随一の展示会です。例年通り、ブースはバルバドスおよびその他カリブ海諸島に拠点を置く販売業者様に限りご利用可能です。私たちの目標は、カリブ海生まれの物品の世界市場を開拓することです。販売業者の皆さまは、金曜日の夜に開催されるオープニング歓迎会で、世界中のバイヤーの方々とぜひご交流ください。出席のご確認は不要です。ご出展者様全員をご招待いたします。

バルバドス国際見本市販売業者様ブース予約フォーム

社名： Shade Tree 工芸社　　　　　　　　　**日付：** 6 月 30 日

連絡先名： Narissa Simpson　　　　　　　　**E メール：** nsimpson@shadetreecrafts.bb

出展ご希望日：　　　　　　　☑ 土曜日　　　　☑ 日曜日

ご希望の展示スペース：

ご希望のスペースがご利用になれない場合に備えて、予備の選択肢をお示しください。

第 1 希望： 89C ブース

第 2 希望： 34A ブース

第 3 希望： 39B ブース

第 4 希望： 75A ブース

ご利用可能な全展示スペースの会場図は、当見本市ウェブサイトにてご確認いただけます。
www.barbadositf.bb/vendormap

```
╔═══════════════════════════════════════════════════════════╗
║            *E メール*                                       ║
╠═══════════════════════════════════════════════════════════╣
║  送信者：   │ Winston Daley、バルバドス国際見本市          │ ║
║  受信者：   │ Narissa Simpson、Shade Tree 工芸社           │ ║
║  日付：     │ 8 月 17 日                                   │ ║
║  件名：     │ ご予約                                       │ ║
╠═══════════════════════════════════════════════════════════╣
```

Simpson 様

バルバドス国際見本市にご参加いただき、ありがとうございます。御社の第 1 希望がすでにご予約済みのため、同イベント用に第 2 希望のブースを予約いたしました。

軽食提供へのご協賛によって、御社に注目を集める機会を活用されることをご検討ください。協賛企業様の社名は、プログラム内および休憩室の看板に大きく掲載されます。詳細と価格設定については、当見本市のウェブサイトにアクセスして「協賛」のリンクをクリックしてください。

イベントでお会いできるのを楽しみにしております。

敬具

Winston Daley
見本市コーディネーター

---

15. 広告は、今年の見本市について何が変更されないままだと示唆していますか。

    (A) 会場の規模
    (B) ブースの割り当て方法
    (C) 招待される販売業者
    (D) イベントの期間

16. 広告では、歓迎会について何が示されていますか。

    (A) 招待客に出席の確認を求めている。
    (B) カリブ海出身のアーティストによる演奏がある。
    (C) 9 月 13 日に開催される予定である。
    (D) 世界中からの販売業者が出席する予定である。

17. Simpson さんについて何が判断できますか。

    (A) ブース代の割引を受ける。
    (B) 昨年、この見本市に参加した。
    (C) 展示日のうちの 1 日に参加できない。
    (D) ある情報を提出し忘れた。

18. Shade Tree 工芸社はどこで製品を展示しますか。

    (A) 34A ブース
    (B) 39B ブース
    (C) 75A ブース
    (D) 89C ブース

19. E メールで、Daley さんは Simpson さんに何をするよう勧めていますか。

    (A) 自社ブースで軽食を出す
    (B) 競合他社を見本市に招待する
    (C) 協賛企業になる
    (D) 販売している製品のリストを彼に送る

Section 9　正解／訳

正解一覧

Part 5	1 (B)	2 (A)	3 (D)	4 (A)	5 (C)	6 (B)	7 (C)
Part 6	8 (D)	9 (A)	10 (C)	11 (B)			
Part 7	12 (A)	13 (C)	14 (C)	15 (B)	16 (B)	17 (D)	18 (C)

Part 5

1. Park さんは Roydon 電機の元上司から郵便で小包を受け取りました。

(A) 〜で
(B) 〜から
(C) 〜なしで
(D) 〜以来

2. 飛行機の手配とホテルの予約は全て、当社の提携旅行代理店 Storg グループを通して行わなくてはなりません。

(A) 手配
(B) 〜を手配する
(C) 〜を手配するための
(D) 〜を手配するだろう

3. 雨が予想されているため、今度の日曜日に計画されている社内ピクニックは屋内に場所を移さなければなりません。

(A) それゆえに
(B) しかしながら
(C) さもなければ
(D) 〜なので

4. 5 月 14 日のウェブサイトの機能向上作業の間、Perry 銀行の顧客は自身のオンライン口座へのアクセスが制限されます。

(A) 彼らの
(B) 彼らを
(C) 彼らは
(D) 彼ら自身

5. Maramigo ホテルの宿泊客は、ホテルのサービスを評価するのに携帯電話アプリを使うことができます。

(A) 〜を描写している
(B) 予定された
(C) 泊まっている
(D) 戻された

6. Ramirez さんの委員会によって可決された予算案には、Fencher 橋の修理のための資金が含まれています。

(A) 起こった
(B) 通過させられた
(C) リラックスした
(D) 伝えられた

7. 事務用椅子は今日配達されましたが、新しい机は月曜日まで届きません。

(A) ひとたび〜すれば
(B) 次に
(C) 〜だけれども
(D) 〜とは違って

Part 6

問題 8-11 は次の E メールに関するものです。

受信者：m.tennyson@yackelartmuseum.co.uk
送信者：l.rivera@pollimail.co.uk
日付：3 月 9 日　月曜日
件名：Re: 新人研修
添付ファイル：Rivera_Bio

Tennyson 様

私はたった今新入社員手続きをオンラインで完了したところですが、問題があるかもしれません。送信ボタンを押したところ、画面が少しの間真っ白になり、メインページに戻ってしまいました。確認メッセージのようなものは何も出ませんでした。私の情報が受信されたことを確かめていただけますか。

また、ウェブサイト用に書くように頼まれた社員紹介を添付しています。用意していただいた書式にできるだけ従うようにしました。*ですが、私の個性もいくらか盛り込みたいと思いました。今、他の皆さんのものを見ていると、他の人のものと違い過ぎているかもしれないと感じています。修正した方がよければお知らせください。

よろしくお願いいたします。

Liam Rivera

---

*問題 10 の挿入文の訳

8. (A) 贈り物
(B) 承認
(C) 支払い
(D) 情報

9. (A) 〜を書くように
(B) それを書くこと
(C) 〜を書いた…
(D) 書かれた

10. (A) 私は彼らの手助けに大いに感謝しています。
(B) 同様に、自分に何ができるか考えてみます。
(C) ですが、私の個性もいくらか盛り込みたいと思いました。
(D) それはインターネット上のどこかで見つかるはずです。

11. (A) 〜を借りる
(B) 〜を修正する
(C) 〜の位置を示す
(D) 〜を保護する

Part 7

問題 12-13 は次のテキストメッセージのやりとりに関するものです。

Julio Sanchez [午後 4 時 02 分]
明日午前の打ち合わせを延期しなければならなくなりそうです。

Sonia McCauley [午後 4 時 04 分]
だめですよ！協議会の準備をするのにそれが必要ですから。

Julio Sanchez [午後 4 時 06 分]
ですが、Nassar さんから先ほど電話がありまして。飛行機が遅れて、彼は明日の夜遅くまで戻れないそうです。

Sonia McCauley [午後 4 時 08 分]
ちょっと聞いてください──今 Ellen Keskinen からメッセージが届きました。明日の午前に顧客にプレゼンをするそうです。彼女は午後まで手が空かず、私はその時間帯は予定が入っています。でも、私たちは本当に全員で集まる必要があります。

Julio Sanchez [午後 4 時 12 分]
協議会は金曜日の午後です。金曜日の午前に私たちは移動ですから、金曜日はだめですね。

Sonia McCauley [午後 4 時 13 分]
えーと。今はもう火曜日の午後です。木曜日はどうですか。同じ時間で。

Julio Sanchez [午後 4 時 14 分]
皆の予定表を確認します。

12. なぜ McCauley さんと Sanchez さんは打ち合わせをしなければならないのですか。

　(A) イベントの計画を立てるため

　(B) 想定外の依頼に対応するため

　(C) 新しいプロジェクトのスタッフを選ぶため

　(D) 顧客の来社に備えるため

13. 午後 4 時 13 分に、McCauley さんは "Same time" という発言で、何を示唆していますか。

　(A) 打ち合わせが協議会とかち合うことに気付いている。

　(B) Keskinen さんが打ち合わせに出られないことを心配している。

　(C) 木曜日の午前にグループの皆に集まってもらいたい。

　(D) 打ち合わせは 1 時間かかると思っている。

問題 14-18 は次のウェブページ、フォーム、E メールに関するものです。

---

https://www.calgaryrenewalcentre.ca/about

カルガリー再生センター（CRC）では、10 年前の設立以来、歴史的建物および建造物の修理・修復を通じた地域社会の向上を自らの使命としてきました。住民や観光客の方々が街を散策して、私たちの文化、社会、建築上の歴史について学んでくださることを私たちは願っています。幸運なことに、私たちの活動のさまざまな分野で支援してくださるボランティアの方々が地域中から集まっています。ボランティアの中には Euclid 通りの事務所で管理業務を手伝ってくださる方や、資金や資材を寄付してくれる民間団体に働きかけてくださる方や、修復作業や地域の歴史に関する専門知識を提供してくださる方もいらっしゃれば、現場で建設作業や大工仕事のお手伝いをしてくださる方もいらっしゃいます。Hanselka 大学建築学部とのパートナーシップにより、建物設計に関する素養をお持ちの方々にもボランティアの機会が新たに開かれています。

私たちは日頃より地元の企業、学校、地域団体からのボランティアチームを喜んでお迎えしております。団体ボランティアのシフトを手配するには、ボランティア登録簿フォームを calgaryrenewalcentre.ca/volunteerform でご提出ください。このフォームに、貴団体がボランティアをするご希望の日時、ご希望の作業の種類を入力してください。詳しくは、当センターのボランティア・コーディネーター Gerald Knoller まで、knoller@calgaryrenewalcentre.ca にご連絡ください。

カルガリー再生センター・ボランティア登録簿

企業名／団体名／学校名： BRH テクノロジー社

申請日： 7 月 10 日

ご希望のボランティア日時： 8 月 12 日、午後 5 時〜午後 8 時

ご希望の作業の種類： 管理業務

名前	E メール	以前に CRC でボランティアのご経験は？	CRC 免責同意書にご署名は？ （全てのボランティアは、CRC がシフトを確認する前に、免責同意書に署名する必要があります。）
Moira Beaulieu	mbeaulieu@brh.ca	はい	はい
Jay Anish	janish@brh.ca	いいえ	はい
Brad Mitsui	bmitsui@brh.ca	いいえ	いいえ
Anika Klum	aklum@brh.ca	はい	はい
Nigel Macomber	nmacomber@brh.ca	はい	はい

送信者：	Alana Moncrief <moncrief@calgaryrenewalcentre.ca>
受信者：	Gerald Knoller <knoller@calgaryrenewalcentre.ca>
件名：	連絡を差し上げてください
日付：	7 月 31 日

お疲れさま、Gerald

8 月に当方でボランティアをしてくださる予定の団体の書類を確認しています。BRH テクノロジー社のチームメンバー 1 名の書類が抜けています。これは、この団体が当センターに来られる前に提出していただく必要があります。できるだけ早く追って連絡を差し上げてください。

よろしくお願いします。

Alana Moncrief
地域活動　部長

---

14. ウェブページによると、CRC の取り組みはどの分野に重点を置いていますか。

(A) 街路や歩道の補修
(B) 環境の保全
(C) 歴史的遺産の保存
(D) 文化的多様性

15. ウェブページは CRC について何を示していますか。

(A) 大学教授によって設立された。
(B) 10 年間、活動している。
(C) 政府からの助成金を受けている。
(D) 近々、他の組織と合併する。

16. BRH テクノロジー社の団体は 8 月 12 日にどこに行くと思われますか。

(A) Hanselka 大学
(B) Euclid 通りの事務所
(C) 寄付団体の本部
(D) 工事現場

17. フォームは Beaulieu さんについて何を示していますか。

(A) BRH テクノロジー社で事務員として働いている。
(B) ボランティアチームのリーダーに選ばれた。
(C) シフトを早めに切り上げなければならない。
(D) 過去に CRC でボランティアをしたことがある。

18. Knoller さんは Moncrief さんから E メールを受信した後、何をすると思われますか。

(A) BRH テクノロジー社のシフトをもっと早い時間帯に変更する
(B) Anish さんを別のチームに配置し直す
(C) Mitsui さんに確認依頼メールを送る
(D) BRH テクノロジー社にチームの人数を増やすよう依頼する

Section 10 正解／訳

正解一覧

Part 5	1 (B)	2 (B)	3 (D)	4 (A)	5 (D)	6 (D)	7 (C)		
Part 6	8 (D)	9 (B)	10 (A)	11 (D)					
Part 7	12 (A)	13 (D)	14 (A)	15 (B)	16 (A)	17 (B)	18 (D)	19 (C)	20 (C)

Part 5

1. 客室乗務員として働く利点のうちの1つは世界を旅行できることです。

(A) 改善
(B) 利点
(C) 遠征
(D) 主題

2. Q-pert ケーブル社は、サービスを4万社を超える新規企業に拡大する計画を発表しました。

(A) 〜を加える
(B) 追加の
(C) 〜を加えること
(D) さらに

3. TKM 放送局は Zhao 氏の著書をテレビシリーズ化し、12月の早い時期に放送することになっています。

(A) 本当に
(B) 正確に
(C) すでに
(D) 早期に

4. 営業担当者が産業見本市に参加する前に、追加の白紙の送り状冊子が注文される予定です。

(A) 〜する前に
(B) どちらか一方の
(C) 〜だが一方
(D) 〜かどうか

5. プロジェクトマネージャーとして、Jeong さんには全ての新規建設計画書を慎重に精査する仕事が課されています。

(A) 慎重な
(B) より慎重な
(C) 慎重さ
(D) 慎重に

6. 新たに開設された工場があるので、Buhr コンクリート社はいまや地域最大の雇用主です。

(A) 〜するとき
(B) 〜まで
(C) 〜であるかのように
(D) 〜のために

7. 月払いのプランが、多くの消費者にとって最も手頃な選択肢かもしれません。

(A) 手頃であること
(B) 供給している
(C) 最も手頃な
(D) より手頃に

Part 6

問題 8-11 は次の広告に関するものです。

Going Native 社のゼリスケープ

低水量庭園の専門会社

ゼリスケープとは、水分がほとんどなくてもお庭で育つ野生植物を用いる庭園デザインの型です。乾燥に強い植物を用いることで限られた水資源を大切に使えます。水の使用量が減れば、水道代も減ります。また、選べる美しい野生植物が非常にたくさんあるので、どなたでも水の使用を減らしながら、鮮やかな色彩と面白い質感に満ちたお庭を楽しむことができます。

Going Native 社は 20 年にわたってゼリスケープを開発しています。*当社の経験豊富なデザイナーは、お客さまの夢のお庭をつくり出すことができます。今すぐ無料相談のお電話を。

---

*問題 11 の挿入文の訳

8. (A) 土壌
(B) 日光
(C) 肥料
(D) 水分

9. (A) 彼を
(B) あなたを
(C) 彼らを
(D) それ自体

10. (A) 〜を減らしている
(B) 〜を減らすために
(C) 彼らは〜を減らした
(D) 〜の削減

11. (A) しかしながら、野生植物へのご要望はありがたく存じます。
(B) 同様に、バラもさまざまな色でご用意できます。
(C) 裏庭にプールがあれば、ご家族全員で楽しめます。
(D) 当社の経験豊富なデザイナーは、お客さまの夢のお庭をつくり出すことができます。

Part 7

問題 12-15 は次の E メールに関するものです。

E メール

受信者：	Lyncett エンタープライズ全従業員
送信者：	Celestina Reese
日付：	3 月 16 日
件名：	図書館は皆さんのためにあります

同僚の皆さん

Lyncett エンタープライズの従業員の特典の 1 つは、社内図書館が提供するサービスを利用できることです。皆さんが思われているかもしれないこととは反対に、当社の図書館はビジネス関連の出版物や文書を所蔵しているだけの場所ではありません。フィクションやノンフィクションの本を幅広く取りそろえているばかりでなく、地方紙各紙やさまざまな人気雑誌も定期購読しています。語学学習ソフトで外国語を学ぶことさえできます！

さらに、お探しのものが当図書館にない場合、入手するお手伝いができるかもしれません。図書館相互貸出制度を使って、他の図書館から当館に書籍を取り寄せることができます。*たった 2 日しかかかりません。

最後に、当館にはご自宅でくつろぎながらご利用できるサービスもあります。例えば、人気の電子書籍をスマートフォンやタブレットなどの各種の個人所有端末で読むことができます。必要なのは、図書館のアプリをダウンロードすることだけです。

図書館のサービスについてご質問がある場合は、当館に内線 251 までご連絡いただくか、3 階にある新しく拡張された図書館スペースにお越しください。

Celestina Reese
図書館利用サービス責任者

*問題 15 の挿入文の訳

12. E メールによると、どれが図書館によって提供されるサービスですか。

    (A) 語学学習教材の利用

    (B) 外国の新聞の定期購読

    (C) 従業員のための研修会

    (D) 従業員がイベントを開催するスペース

13. なぜ Reese さんは図書館のアプリについて述べていますか。

    (A) 料金の引き上げを説明するため

    (B) 技術的な問題への注意喚起をするため

    (C) 図書館で行われる変更点を知らせるため

    (D) どうすれば従業員が電子書籍を利用できるか説明するため

14. Reese さんは図書館について何を示していますか。

    (A) 同館のスペースは最近拡張された。

    (B) 近々開館時間を変更する。

    (C) 従業員は同館から電子機器を借りることができる。

    (D) 同館の司書は全員パートタイムで働いている。

15. [1]、[2]、[3]、[4] と記載された箇所のうち、次の文が入るのに最もふさわしいのはどれですか。

「たった 2 日しかかかりません」

    (A) [1]

    (B) [2]

    (C) [3]

    (D) [4]

問題 16-20 は次の広告と 2 通の E メールに関するものです。

Fronteras and Company

ご家族皆さまのファッション・ニーズの全てがそろっています！

10 月の特別セール

店舗とオンラインにて有効。オンラインでは、下記の割引コードを
ご利用の上、割引を受けてください。

10％割引　ワンピース
利用コード：OCTFORM71

20％割引　服飾品全品（帽子を除く）
利用コード：OCTACC43

30％割引　子ども服
利用コード：OCTCHIL29

75 ドルを超えるご注文で、お買い物用エコバッグを無料プレゼント！
1 回のご注文につき割引コードは 1 点に限りご利用になれます。

送信者：	Ameena Almasi <aalmasi@rhyta.com.au>
受信者：	Fronteras and Company カスタマーサービス <custserv@fronteras.com.au>
日付：	10 月 16 日　火曜日　午前 6 時 44 分
件名：	割引注文コード

こんにちは。

つい先ほど、そちらのホームページで男児用シャツ 3 枚をオンライン注文しようとしました。ところが、割引コードを入力しようとすると、そのコードが無効だというエラーメッセージが表示されました。私はコードを正しく入力していることを確認するために 3 回試してみました。助けてもらえませんか。どうしても今日シャツを注文して、10 月 20 日より前に商品を受け取りたいのです。その日は子どもの誕生日パーティーがある日なのです。

よろしくお願いします。

Ameena Almasi

送信者：	Fronteras and Company カスタマーサービス <custserv@fronteras.com.au>
受信者：	Ameena Almasi <aalmasi@rhyta.com.au>
日付：	10 月 16 日　火曜日　午前 11 時 04 分
件名：	RE: 割引注文コード

Almasi 様

E メールを頂き、ありがとうございます。弊社ウェブサイトでのご注文に問題があったとのことで、申し訳ございません。お調べしましたところ、広告に誤ったコードが記載されていたことが分かりました。ご不便をおかけいたしましたことをおわび申し上げます。問題は解決いたしましたので、現在は広告に記載されているコードをご使用になれます。

今回の件は全面的に当方の落ち度でございますので、追加料金なしで速達便を手配いたしました。おっしゃっていたパーティーの前日には、ご注文品をお受け取りいただける見込みです。

他にお困りのことやご不明点がおありでしたら、ご遠慮なく E メールをお送りいただくか、弊社カスタマーサービスまでお電話ください。

敬具

Sheldon Blythe
Fronteras and Company カスタマーサービス担当

Section 10

16. Fronteras and Company はどんな種類の事業ですか。

(A) 衣料品店
(B) 広告代理店
(C) パーティー企画会社
(D) 電子機器店

17. 顧客はどうすれば無料のバッグをもらう資格を得られますか。

(A) アンケート調査に答えることによって
(B) 最低金額のお金を使うことによって
(C) 10 月 15 日までに注文することによって
(D) 優良顧客サービスに申し込むことによって

18. Almasi さんは注文に対してどれくらいの割引を受けるつもりでしたか。

(A) 5 パーセント
(B) 10 パーセント
(C) 20 パーセント
(D) 30 パーセント

19. なぜ Almasi さんはうまく注文ができなかったのですか。

(A) 店にその商品がなかったから
(B) あまりに多くの人がそのウェブサイトを利用していたから
(C) 広告に誤りがあったから
(D) 1 台の機械が故障したから

20. いつ Almasi さんは注文品を受け取ると思われますか。

(A) 10 月 16 日
(B) 10 月 17 日
(C) 10 月 19 日
(D) 10 月 20 日

正解一覧

Part 5	1 (D)	2 (C)	3 (A)	4 (B)	5 (D)	6 (A)	7 (C)		
Part 6	8 (A)	9 (B)	10 (C)	11 (B)					
Part 7	12 (A)	13 (D)	14 (C)	15 (B)	16 (D)	17 (B)	18 (B)	19 (A)	20 (B)

Part 5

1. CEO は役員たちに向けて話しましたが、彼らは彼が引退を表明するとは予想していませんでした。

(A) 〜だが、それらは
(B) 〜だが、彼らの
(C) 〜すること
(D) 〜だが、彼らは

2. 編集職として検討されるためには、応募者は金曜日までに履歴書を提出しなければなりません。

(A) 場合
(B) 解決策
(C) 職
(D) 態度

3. Steinhart and Sons 社の利益は前四半期に急激な減少を示しました。

(A) 利益
(B) 〜を稼ぐ［動詞の原形／現在形］
(C) 〜を稼いだ
(D) 〜を稼ぐ［動詞の三人称単数現在形］

4. 当社の誰でも、当社新製品の実演に自由に参加できます。

(A)（〜する）人々
(B) 誰でも
(C) お互い
(D) どれでも

5. 地元の会社員たちは、対応が速くて食べ物の価格が手頃なため、Vasalisa's カフェが気に入っています。

(A) 経済的な
(B) 〜を節約する
(C) 経済
(D) 経済的に

6. Argenca 社の新料金プランは、さらなる顧客を呼び込むための戦略的な動きです。

(A) 戦略的な
(B) 予防可能な
(C) 遠方の
(D) 以前の

7. 全ての支払いは、税法規の順守を確実にするために徹底的に確認されなければなりません。

(A) 熱望して
(B) 一般に
(C) 徹底的に
(D) ほとんど

Part 6

問題 8-11 は次の記事に関するものです。

Rite ショップの店舗が新たなコラボレーション商品を発売

全国的な食料品チェーン Rite ショップはつい先頃、他にはない商品で知られている幾つかの食品専門ブランドとの提携を発表した。こうした商品の中には Gerry のチーズ、H&R のベーグル、Daily Bread のパンや焼き菓子などが含まれる。これらのブランド商品は、厳選された Rite ショップの店舗で近日中に販売される予定だ。*今後数カ月の間には、全店舗がこれらの商品の販売を開始する。

「お客さまは Rite ショップでこうしたブランド商品を目にすれば、とても喜ぶと思います」と、CEO の Natalie Yalbirs は水曜日の記者会見で述べた。「そして、私たち Rite ショップの従業員は販売商品の幅を広げるこの機会に胸を高鳴らせています」。

---

*問題 10 の挿入文の訳

8. (A) 知られている
　　(B) 〜を知っている…
　　(C) 彼らは〜を知っている
　　(D) 知られていた

9. (A) いまでも
　　(B) 近いうちに
　　(C) 同様に
　　(D) これまでに

10. (A) それにもかかわらず、ホットコーヒーはいまや全店舗で購入できる。
　　(B) Rite ショップは 25 年以上前に創立された。
　　(C) 今後数カ月の間には、全店舗がこれらの商品の販売を開始する。
　　(D) 例えば、Daily Bread は地元で営業している。

11. (A) 予算
　　(B) 売り物
　　(C) 倉庫
　　(D) 会員数

Part 7

問題 12-15 は次のテキストメッセージのやりとりに関するものです。

Annabelle Marder（午前 11 時 12 分） こんにちは、Preeti、Kwesi。文化遺産フェスティバル実行委員会がイベントのためにまだ私のバンドと契約したいと思っているかどうか知りたいのですが。

Preeti Sandhu（午前 11 時 15 分） こんにちは、Annabelle。そのはずですが、たぶん Kwesi がそれを確認できると思いますよ。今回は彼が公演アーティストの契約担当なのです、私ではなくて。

Annabelle Marder（午前 11 時 17 分） 分かりました。ただ、早くお返事をもらえるとありがたいです。私たちは新しいアルバム制作に取り組んでいて、6 月 26 日の週末に録音スタジオに空きがあるのです。

Preeti Sandhu（午前 11 時 18 分） つまり、私たちのイベント開催時ですね。分かりました。

Kwesi Asiamah（午前 11 時 20 分） こんにちは、Annabelle！ ずっとあなたに連絡しようと思っていたのです。実際、私たちはとても契約をお願いしたいと思っています。あなたのバンドは 2 年前のフェスティバルで大きな注目を集めました。昨年はサルサとレゲエをミックスしたあなた方の独特の音楽を聞けなくて寂しかったです。

Preeti Sandhu（午前 11 時 24 分） ええ、<u>あなた方が来られなくて残念でした。</u>

Annabelle Marder（午前 11 時 25 分） 私の記憶が正しければ、外せない別の約束があったのです。私たちもそれを残念に思いました。

Kwesi Asiamah（午前 11 時 26 分） では、公演スケジュールを確認次第、あなたに関連情報を全てお送りします。明日でも間に合いますか。

Annabelle Marder（午前 11 時 27 分） 明日で大丈夫です。スタジオと相談して別の空き時間枠を見つける時間が確保できますから。ご連絡を楽しみに待っています。

12. Marder さんについて何が示されていますか。

(A) スケジュールがかち合うことを心配している。

(B) フェスティバルの公演者を雇う担当である。

(C) フェスティバルの実行委員会に属している。

(D) 本の執筆に取り組んでいる。

13. 文化遺産フェスティバルについて示唆されていないことは何ですか。

(A) ライブ音楽を呼び物にしている。

(B) 6 月に開催される予定である。

(C) 毎年行われる。

(D) 入場にはチケットが必要である。

14. 午前 11 時 24 分に、Sandhu さんは "it's too bad you couldn't make it" という発言で、何を意味していますか。

(A) イベントへの交通手段が利用できなかった。

(B) スタジオ録音が中止になった。

(C) Marder さんのバンドがイベントに参加できなかったことを残念に思っている。

(D) Marder さんのバンドがまだレゲエ音楽を演奏していればよいのにと思っている。

15. Asiamah さんは何をすると約束していますか。

(A) スタジオに連絡する

(B) さらなる詳細情報を提供する

(C) Marder さんと会う

(D) 契約を更新する

Section

11

問題 16-20 は次の計画書、予定表、地図に関するものです。

計画書：Hoek 社コミュニティーガーデン事業

概要：現在進められている地域支援事業の一環として、Hoek 社は当社倉庫所在地に近接する Ostend 地区のコミュニティーガーデンを支援します。当社は景観設計家 Todor Jansen に空間の設計を依頼しましたが、造園は社員ボランティアが行うことになります。ガーデンの立ち上げ花壇の暫定予算は以下をご参照ください。

数量	品目	費用（単価）
24	板〔3 メートル〕	12 ユーロ 25 セント
24	板〔4 メートル〕	15 ユーロ 75 セント
3	ボックス固定くぎ〔20 センチ〕	8 ユーロ 50 セント
16	金属製留め具	2 ユーロ 99 セント
16	木製コーナー支柱〔2 メートル〕	10 ユーロ

**Ostend コミュニティーガーデン
ボランティア予定表（チーム 1）**

・週末 1（3 月 18 〜 19 日）：やぶを刈り払う、地面をならす

・週末 2（3 月 25 〜 26 日）：花壇の木枠を組み立てる、木枠を所定の場所に設置する

・週末 3（4 月 1 〜 2 日）：土と肥料を入れる、最初の種をまく

・週末 4（4 月 8 〜 9 日）：苗に水をやって間引きする、チーム 2 が行う庭の手入れスケジュールを決める

Ostend コミュニティーガーデン 地図
(植え付け開始日を付記)

花壇 1
レタス (4 月 1 日)
エンドウ豆 (4 月 15 日)

花壇 2
イチゴ (4 月 15 日)
ブルーベリー (4 月 29 日)

花壇 3
カボチャ (6 月 3 日)
芽キャベツ (6 月 10 日)

花壇 4
トウモロコシ (7 月 1 日)
豆 (7 月 15 日)

---

16. コミュニティーガーデンはどこに位置する予定ですか。

(A) 市の公園の中
(B) オフィスビルの向かい
(C) 工場の隣
(D) 保管施設の近く

17. 計画書によると、立ち上げ花壇を作るのに何本のコーナー支柱が必要ですか。

(A) 4 本
(B) 16 本
(C) 20 本
(D) 24 本

18. Hoek 社はいつまでに予算にある資材を購入する必要がありますか。

(A) 週末 1
(B) 週末 2
(C) 週末 3
(D) 週末 4

19. チーム 1 のボランティアはガーデンに何を植える予定ですか。

(A) レタス
(B) エンドウ豆
(C) トウモロコシ
(D) カボチャ

20. 地図によると、ガーデンボランティアはどこに 2 種類の果物を植える予定ですか。

(A) 花壇 1
(B) 花壇 2
(C) 花壇 3
(D) 花壇 4

正解一覧

Part 5	1 (A)	2 (C)	3 (C)	4 (D)	5 (B)	6 (C)	7 (A)
Part 6	8 (B)	9 (B)	10 (A)	11 (D)			
Part 7	12 (A)	13 (B)	14 (B)	15 (A)	16 (B)	17 (D)	18 (C)

Part 5

1. Iashvili さんの退職パーティーは Blue マリーナ・グリルという、海岸沿いにある人気のレストランで行われます。

    (A) 人気のある
    (B) 仮の
    (C) 多数の
    (D) 絶え間ない

2. Cardenas 産業社は、新たな決済システムを導入するに際してお客さまのご理解とご協力をお願いいたします。

    (A) 協力する
    (B) 協力した
    (C) 協力
    (D) 協力して

3. Wong さんはその職をひとまず引き受けましたが、後になって詳細不明の理由により辞退しました。

    (A) 準備
    (B) 食糧
    (C) 暫定的に
    (D) 暫定的な

4. 保育施設での Lampron さんの職務の 1 つは職員の予定表を作成することです。

    (A) 〜を教育する
    (B) 〜を許可する
    (C) 〜を投資する
    (D) 〜を作り出す

5. 塗料の製造では、多くの原料をさまざまな割合で混ぜ合わせる必要があります。

    (A) 〜に接して
    (B) 〜の状態で
    (C) 〜の後に
    (D) 〜を超えて

6. Selman さんは 5 月 24 日にイスタンブールへ出発し、5 月 30 日に戻る予定です。

    (A) 戻った
    (B) 戻ること
    (C) 戻る
    (D) 戻される

7. Villadsen 社の携帯電話には、通常のメーカー保証に加え、2 年間の破損保証が付いています。

    (A) 〜に加えて
    (B) 〜に先立って
    (C) 〜の場合に備えて
    (D) 〜に近い

Part 6

問題 8-11 は次のメモに関するものです。

差出人：Sergio L. McGovern　事業担当副社長
宛先：フロア監督者各位
件名：検査
日付：6 月 3 日

製品の品質向上と国内規制の順守を確実にする取り組みの一環として、全製造ユニットが、直ちに実施される無作為検査の対象となります。この検査は Venturia システム社の技術者によって行われます。彼らは製造ラインを監視し、倉庫作業を観察します。検査官は予告なしで到着することをご承知おきください。すなわち、彼らはいつ何時でも立ち入る可能性があります。検査官が作業を完了する間、皆さんは通常どおり作業を続けるようお願いします。各検査の 1 週間以内に、詳細な報告書が私のところに直接送られてきます。*あなた方も同様にコピーを受け取ることになります。よろしくお願いします。

---

*問題 11 の挿入文の訳

8. (A) 〜を向上させている
　　(B) 〜を向上させるための
　　(C) 〜を向上させた…
　　(D) 向上の〜

9. (A) 〜だった
　　(B) 〜であろう
　　(C) 〜になっていた
　　(D) 〜であるところだった

10. (A) 警告
　　(B) 遅延
　　(C) 許可
　　(D) 宿泊設備

11. (A) 完了次第、評価書を提出してください。
　　(B) 合意した時間に速やかにお越しください。
　　(C) 検査官は受付で記名します。
　　(D) あなた方も同様にコピーを受け取ることになります。

Part 7

問題 12-13 は次の記事に関するものです。

Tiff 川の最新情報

コーデール（4 月 30 日）── Tiff 川一帯は、West 渓谷鉄道路線の通勤客にとって長い間目障りだったが、7 月 1 日の自然公園としての開園に先立ち、再生工事の最終段階に入っている。

プロジェクトが承認されてから今週で 2 年目となるが、工事が始まったのは 1 月に入ってからだ。この地域には、かつて産業用ガラス工場があった。

コーデール市長 Ed Scala は今日、作業員は 6 月までに野草の植え付けを完了する見込みだと発表した。作業員はすでに古いコンクリートやアスファルトを撤去し、川のごみを除去し、既存の土を砂に置き換えた。

12. 再生工事はいつ始まりましたか。

    (A) 1 月

    (B) 4 月

    (C) 6 月

    (D) 7 月

13. 記事によると、次に何が起こりますか。

    (A) 工場が修理される。

    (B) 草が植え付けられる。

    (C) 鉄道駅が完成する。

    (D) 土が入れ換えられる。

問題 14-18 は次の記事、コメントカード、オンラインレビューフォームに関するものです。

コーク県コーブ（2月15日）——コーブ町は、4月28日（土）に初の地域フェアを主催する。主催者によると、フェアには、コーブだけでなくコーク港沿いの近隣の町からも企業や地域団体が出店する予定だ。このイベントは無料で一般公開され、ブースは町の3カ所の中心地にまとまって設置される。

「私たちの目標の1つは、皆さんに町が提供する特別な場所全てに立ち寄ってもらうことです」とイベントコーディネーターの Caoimhe Carroll は話す。「地元の企業や事業に関する情報ブースが Cobh 彫刻公園の外に設置され、食べ物の屋台が近くの Cobh 音楽堂の駐車場に並び、アート作品の出店者が港沿いのあちこちに店を出します。皆さんにこの地域の探索を楽しんでいただきたいですね」。

参加を希望する出店者は www.cobhcommunityfair.ie で申し込みができる。4月より前に登録した人は地元企業で使えるクーポンが入ったトートバッグがもらえる。

コーブ地域フェアの出店者として
体験談をお聞かせください！

お名前： Joanna Harbro

事業者名： Joabro 宝飾品店

フェアのニュース記事が出てすぐに登録しました。このイベントに参加できることにわくわくしたからです！ 来場者の方たちとのおしゃべりは本当に楽しかったですし、在庫品をたくさん売りました！ ただ、来場者の方々はもっと多くのアーティストが参加することを期待していたのではないかと思います。次回のフェアの前に、さらなる働きかけや宣伝活動をすれば、おそらくもっと多くの出店者に参加してもらえるでしょう。

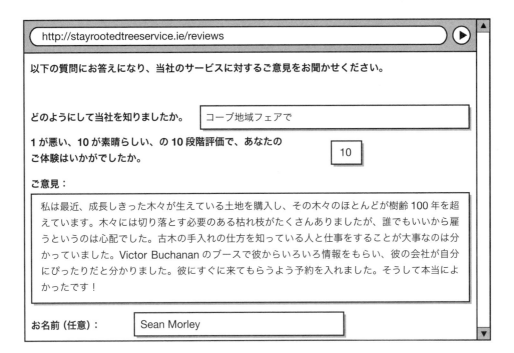

http://stayrootedtreeservice.ie/reviews

以下の質問にお答えになり、当社のサービスに対するご意見をお聞かせください。

どのようにして当社を知りましたか。　　　コーブ地域フェアで

1 が悪い、10 が素晴らしい、の 10 段階評価で、あなたの
ご体験はいかがでしたか。　　　　　　　　　　10

ご意見：

私は最近、成長しきった木々が生えている土地を購入し、その木々のほとんどが樹齢 100 年を超えています。木々には切り落とす必要のある枯れ枝がたくさんありましたが、誰でもいいから雇うというのは心配でした。古木の手入れの仕方を知っている人と仕事をすることが大事なのは分かっていました。Victor Buchanan のブースで彼からいろいろ情報をもらい、彼の会社が自分にぴったりだと分かりました。彼にすぐに来てもらうよう予約を入れました。そうして本当によかったです！

お名前（任意）：　　　Sean Morley

---

14. 記事によると、なぜフェアの主催者は出店者たちを異なる場所に配置しましたか。

(A) 運動を促すため
(B) 観光を促進するため
(C) 交通渋滞を最小限に抑えるため
(D) 駐車場の制約に対応するため

15. Harbro さんについて、何が示唆されていますか。

(A) 早期登録のプレゼントをもらった。
(B) 登録料の割引を受ける資格があった。
(C) ニュース記事で取り上げられた。
(D) 自分のブースの場所を選ぶことができた。

16. コメントカードで、Harbro さんは今後のイベントのために何を提案していますか。

(A) フェア会場周辺にもっと分かりやすい看板を掲示すること
(B) アート作品の出店者をもっと募集すること
(C) ブースの設営を手助けすること
(D) 商品展示のより良い選択肢を提供すること

17. Buchanan さんについて、何が示唆されていますか。

(A) フェアを企画運営した。
(B) フェアで食べ物を売った。
(C) 土曜日にコーブに通っている。
(D) Cobh 彫刻公園の外でブースを出していた。

18. オンラインレビューフォームによると、何がMorley さんの優先事項でしたか。

(A) 即日サービスを提供できること
(B) 地元で長く仕事をしてきた実績
(C) 樹齢が高い木々の手入れをした経験
(D) 切り落とした枝を快く撤去してくれること

正解一覧

Part 5	1 (C)	2 (D)	3 (D)	4 (B)	5 (A)	6 (C)	7 (B)
Part 6	8 (C)	9 (B)	10 (B)	11 (D)			
Part 7	12 (C)	13 (A)	14 (B)	15 (C)	16 (A)	17 (D)	18 (A)

Part 5

1. Thayerton 商工会議所のウェブサイトには、町の全事業者を網羅した一覧が載っています。

(A) 〜を含む［動詞の原形／現在形］
(B) 〜を含んでいる
(C) 〜を含む［動詞の三人称単数現在形］
(D) 〜を含むための

2. Paek さんは丁寧な顧客サービスの重要性について論じる予定です。

(A) 〜へ
(B) 〜で
(C) 〜による
(D) 〜の

3. その建物に新しい棟を増築する計画は順調に進んでいます。

(A) 順調な
(B) 滑らかさ
(C) 滑らかにすること
(D) 順調に

4. Barrios 博士は入所したばかりですが、すでに当事務所のために 12 のクライアントを獲得しています。

(A) 〜するときはいつでも
(B) 〜だけれども
(C) 〜した後で
(D) ひとたび〜すれば

5. 新しい家具は、会社ロビーへの心地よい追加要素となっています。

(A) 喜びを与えるような
(B) 喜んで
(C) 喜び
(D) 喜びを与えるもの

6. 投資家からの資金を確保するために、当社の商品に対する確固たる潜在市場があることを示さなければなりません。

(A) 〜を与えないでおく
(B) 〜を強く望む
(C) 〜を確保する
(D) 〜を実施する

7. Hobrock さんは町の新しいイタリア料理店を非常に高く評価しています。

(A) 〜に関して
(B) 好感
(C) 評価された
(D) 敬意の念

Part 6

問題 8-11 は次の記事に関するものです。

フロリダ州ターポンスプリングス（6 月 24 日）──開館以来初めて、Tarpon Springs 美術館は著名な地元アーティスト Nikos Parios の作品を展示する。この回顧展は 7 月の間中開催される予定だ。

Parios さんは 7 月 1 日夜に行われる回顧展初日の式典に出席する。しかしながら、今回展示される作品全てが彼のものというわけではない。Parios さんの下で学んだ若手アーティスト 4 人の作品も出展される。*このアーティストたちも 7 月 1 日に Parios さんと同席する予定だ。

回顧展は先頃の美術館改装以来、初めて開催される展覧会となる。常連の来館者であれば、壁の壁画が修復され、大きな天窓が設置されたことに気付くだろう。

Section
13

8. (A) ～を展示してきた
(B) ～を展示する
(C) ～を展示する予定である
(D) ～を展示した

9. (A) それの
(B) 彼のもの
(C) 彼女のもの
(D) 彼らのもの

10. (A) Parios さんは若いときに絵を描き始めた。
(B) このアーティストたちも 7 月 1 日に Parios さんと同席する予定だ。
(C) Parios さんはターポンスプリングスで生まれた。
(D) 一つの壁画は Parios さんによって描かれた。

11. (A) 前述の
(B) 初期の
(C) 公的な
(D) 常連の

Part 7

問題 12-13 は次のテキストメッセージのやりとりに関するものです。

Shekeia Jacobs（午前 9 時 04 分）

お疲れさまです。ビデオ会議に接続したのですが、他に誰もつながっていませんでした。会議の日付が変更されたとき、電話番号かダイヤルインコードも変更されましたか。

Karl Rudd（午前 9 時 05 分）

会議は今日の 10 時からです。当初は 9 時からの予定でしたが、日付を変更したときに開始時刻も変えました。最新情報をお送りするのを忘れていて申し訳ありません。

Shekeia Jacobs（午前 9 時 07 分）

大丈夫ですよ。ダイヤルイン情報は同じですか。

Karl Rudd（午前 9 時 08 分）

はい。

Shekeia Jacobs（午前 9 時 09 分）

ありがとう。会議を逃したわけではなかったので、ひとまずよかったです。では、後ほどビデオ会議で！

12. なぜJacobsさんはRuddさんに連絡しましたか。

    (A) 彼に推薦をするため

    (B) ダイヤルインコードを変更するため

    (C) 会議について尋ねるため

    (D) ビデオ通話を中止するため

13. 午前 9 時 07 分に、Jacobs さんは "It's fine" という発言で、何を意味していると思われますか。

    (A) 新しい開始時刻は彼女にとって受け入れられるものである。

    (B) 参加者名簿は最終的なものである。

    (C) 彼女は会議の場所に賛成している。

    (D) 彼女は最新の電話機器を気に入っている。

Section
13

問題 14-18 は次の E メールと表に関するものです。

＊E メール＊

受信者：	学部長各位
送信者：	大学図書館システム部長　Dorit Perez
日付：	5 月 2 日
件名：	ノートパソコン貸出コーナー
添付ファイル：	📎 設置場所の表

皆さんもすでにご存じのとおり、約 1 年前に Shelburne 大学図書館に設置されたノートパソコン自動貸出コーナーは学生に好評です。図書館のこのメインの貸出コーナーは、一日 24 時間ノートパソコンを利用できる簡単で安全な手段を提供しています。学生が大学課程に正式に登録されている限り、学生証のチップを読み取るだけで、貸出機が鍵付きのボックスからノートパソコンを出します。図書館の貸出返却カウンターのスタッフは、もはや時間のかかる貸出手続きで学生を補助する必要がないので、他の業務に従事できます。

図書館システム部のこの成功により、今月末からこの構想を学内の他の場所にも拡大することにしました。表が示しているように、新設の自動貸出コーナーのノートパソコン台数は、予想使用量に応じて数が変わります。リスト上の最後の場所は暫定的なもので、施設部の予算の承認待ちですので、ご注意ください。来月後半には運用開始となる見込みです。

ご質問やご不明な点がありましたら、私までご連絡ください。

ノートパソコン貸出コーナーの場所	稼働時間	ノートパソコン台数
学生会館	午前 8:00 ― 午後 10:00	20
健康科学センター	午前 8:00 ― 午後 6:00	20
工学科	午前 8:00 ― 午後 6:00	36
経済産業研究所	午前 8:00 ― 午後 10:00	30
言語学部	午前 10:00 ― 午後 5:00	15

14. 昨年、Shelburne 大学によって何の措置が講じられましたか。

(A) 図書館スタッフの追加雇用

(B) 貸出方法の簡易化

(C) 図書館内への教室の設置

(D) 新キャンパスの開校

15. 大学図書館のノートパソコン貸出コーナーについて何が示されていますか。

(A) 本の返却に使える。

(B) 貸出返却カウンターの隣にある。

(C) 24 時間利用できる。

(D) 正常に機能していない。

16. E メールの第 1 段落 6 行目にある "attend to" に最も意味が近いのは

(A) 〜に対処する

(B) 〜と仲良くする

(C) 〜を待ち受ける

(D) 〜に訴える

17. 表は工学科のノートパソコン貸出コーナーについて何を示唆していますか。

(A) 6 月にオープンする。

(B) キャンパスの中心部から遠い。

(C) 2 機種のノートパソコンを提供する。

(D) 比較的人気が高いと予想されている。

18. Perez さんは施設部が何を承認することを見越していますか。

(A) 言語学部のノートパソコン貸出コーナー

(B) ノートパソコン貸出コーナーの安全対策の強化

(C) 稼働時間の延長

(D) 学生証の更新

正解一覧

Part 5	1 (D)	2 (B)	3 (B)	4 (A)	5 (A)	6 (D)	7 (B)
Part 6	8 (D)	9 (A)	10 (D)	11 (C)			
Part 7	12 (D)	13 (A)	14 (D)	15 (C)	16 (B)	17 (A)	18 (A)

Part 5

1. ページ番号が正しくなかったので、Tran さんはそのパンフレットを印刷所に送り返しました。

(A) 使用者
(B) 大国
(C) タイマー
(D) 番号

2. Becker さんは、人を率いる生まれつきの才能があるため、副社長に選ばれました。

(A) 本質
(B) 生来の
(C) 生来
(D) 自然らしさ

3. Amsel 配管社は、経営陣に変更があったにもかかわらず、良い業績を上げています。

(A) 〜の内部に
(B) 〜にもかかわらず
(C) 〜の向かいに
(D) 〜の下に

4. メディアコンサルティング会社 Greensap グループは、貴社のビジネス上の働きかけの課題に対する解決策をご提供することができます。

(A) 〜を提供する
(B) 提供者
(C) 提供
(D) 提供された

5. Tramont 建設社は、最高品質の建設資材を使用しています。

(A) 最高の
(B) 改良された
(C) 魅力的な
(D) 積極的な

6. 休日の前日には、Pham さんは通常、従業員が1時間早く帰ることを認めています。

(A) 〜を一般化する
(B) 一般化
(C) 一般的な
(D) 通常

7. 冬期が寒冷な地域の小売店経営者はしばしば、そうした季節の間の売り上げの減少に気付きます。

(A) 期間
(B) 減少
(C) 取引
(D) 乗車

Part 6

問題 8-11 は次のメモに関するものです。

宛先：従業員各位
差出人：Martha Bauer
件名：会議
日付：4 月 4 日

生産性の向上を図るため、私たちは自社内における情報伝達の最も効果的な方法を分析してきました。その結果、毎月開かれる会議の回数を減らす努力をすることを決定しました。この目的のため、今後、従業員の皆さんが会議の予定を立てる際は、一般ガイドラインを順守するようお願いいたします。このガイドラインには、いかなる会議も常に詳細な議題を書くことと、会議の具体的な終了時刻を明記することが盛り込まれています。さらに、従業員は本人の出席が不可欠な場合にのみ会議に呼ばれるべきです。*出席する必要がない場合は、招待を辞退しましょう。このガイドラインに従うことで、私たち全員が自分の業務に取り組むためのより多くの時間を確保できるようになることを期待しています。

*問題 11 の挿入文の訳

Section

14

8. (A) 〜の近くに
   (B) 〜に反対して
   (C) 〜の後で
   (D) 〜の内部で

9. (A) その結果
   (B) そうであっても
   (C) 一方で
   (D) その代わりに

10. (A) 〜を求めている
    (B) 〜を求めた
    (C) 〜を求める［動詞の三人称単数現在形］
    (D) 〜を求める［動詞の一人称複数現在形］

11. (A) 明日の会合は講堂で行われます。
    (B) 最新の議題が別途送られます。
    (C) 出席する必要がない場合は、招待を辞退しましょう。
    (D) 手助けが可能な場合は、私に E メールを送ってください。

Part 7

問題 12-13 は次の E メールに関するものです。

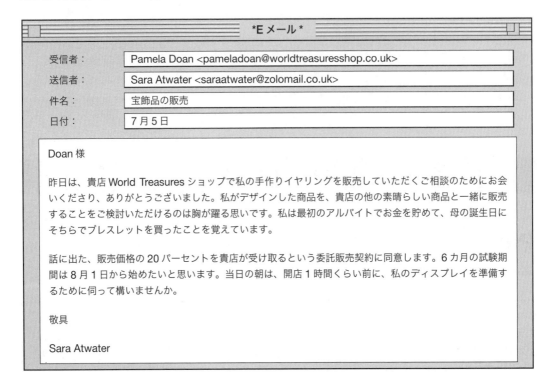

＊E メール＊	

受信者：	Pamela Doan <pameladoan@worldtreasuresshop.co.uk>
送信者：	Sara Atwater <saraatwater@zolomail.co.uk>
件名：	宝飾品の販売
日付：	7 月 5 日

Doan 様

昨日は、貴店 World Treasures ショップで私の手作りイヤリングを販売していただくご相談のためにお会いくださり、ありがとうございました。私がデザインした商品を、貴店の他の素晴らしい商品と一緒に販売することをご検討いただけるのは胸が躍る思いです。私は最初のアルバイトでお金を貯めて、母の誕生日にそちらでブレスレットを買ったことを覚えています。

話に出た、販売価格の 20 パーセントを貴店が受け取るという委託販売契約に同意します。6 カ月の試験期間は 8 月 1 日から始めたいと思います。当日の朝は、開店 1 時間くらい前に、私のディスプレイを準備するために伺って構いませんか。

敬具

Sara Atwater

12. Atwater さんについて何が示されていますか。

(A) 以前、World Treasures ショップで働いたことがある。

(B) 自分の店で World Treasures ショップの商品を販売している。

(C) World Treasures ショップの求人に応募している。

(D) World Treasures ショップのかつての顧客である。

13. Atwater さんは何を要望していますか。

(A) 店に行くことのできる時間

(B) 利益の 20 パーセントの取り分

(C) 最初の試用期間の延長

(D) 使用可能なもっと広い展示スペース

問題 14-18 は次の 2 通の E メールに関するものです。

受信者：	williamc@sunmail.ca
送信者：	reservations@goldflagairways.ca
件名：	Gold Flag 航空——お知らせ
日付：	6 月 1 日

セクション 1：予約 849207
乗客名：William Conners
マイレージ ID：36B117

セクション 2：航空便 GF2465
出発地：YVR、バンクーバー、
　ブリティッシュコロンビア州、カナダ
日時：6 月 7 日、14:40
目的地：ICN、ソウル、韓国
到着時刻：17:50
座席：エコノミークラス 28C

セクション 3：航空便 GF3400
出発地：ICN、ソウル、韓国
日時：6 月 12 日、15:30
目的地：YVR、バンクーバー、
　ブリティッシュコロンビア州、カナダ
到着時刻：9:20
座席：エコノミークラス 31A

セクション 4：方針
航空券の詳細について、この E メールをよくお読みください。搭乗者の名前が、旅行者の身元確認書に記載されているものと完全に一致していることをご確認ください。修正が必要な場合は当社まで、reservations@goldflagairways.ca に E メールをお送りください。この情報に対するいかなる変更のご依頼も、フライト時刻に先立って、少なくとも 48 時間前に受領される必要があります。

E メールメッセージ

受信者：	Gold Flag 航空 <reservations@goldflagairways.ca>
送信者：	William Conner <williamc@sunmail.ca>
日付：	6 月 2 日
件名：	予約 849207

予約 849207 について誤りがありますので、ご注意ください。私の姓は航空券に Conner と記載されているべきです。航空券上の私の姓のつづりは現状では間違っています。

また、私のマイレージアカウントに貯まっているトラベルポイントで、座席区分をビジネスクラスにアップグレードできるかどうかを教えてください。

敬具

William Conner

14. 1 通目の E メールの目的は何ですか。

(A) マイレージ会員であることを確認すること

(B) 新しい航空会社を宣伝すること

(C) スケジュールの変更を説明すること

(D) 航空券購入の詳細を知らせること

15. Gold Flag 航空について何が示唆されていますか。

(A) 予約情報の変更には手数料が請求される。

(B) キャンセルには少なくとも 24 時間前の通知が必要である。

(C) バンクーバーとソウル間の直行便を提供している。

(D) 低予算旅行者に人気がある。

16. Conner さんについて何が示唆されていますか。

(A) 就職面接のために旅行しようとしている。

(B) 過去に Gold Flag 航空で旅行したことがある。

(C) 航空券の割引を依頼したいと思っている。

(D) 特別な手荷物の要望がある。

17. 1 通目の E メールのどのセクションに問題が含まれていますか。

(A) セクション 1

(B) セクション 2

(C) セクション 3

(D) セクション 4

18. 2 通目の E メールの第 2 段落 1 行目にある "informed" に最も意味が近いのは

(A) 通知されて

(B) 提案されて

(C) 教育されて

(D) 指示されて

Section 15 正解／訳

正解一覧

Part 5	1 (B)	2 (A)	3 (A)	4 (B)	5 (D)	6 (C)	7 (D)	
Part 6	8 (C)	9 (B)	10 (A)	11 (D)				
Part 7	12 (C)	13 (B)	14 (A)	15 (B)	16 (C)	17 (D)	18 (B)	19 (A)

Part 5

1. 大工見習いへの受け入れは、応募者のこれまでの
経歴次第です。

(A) ～を受け入れる
(B) 受け入れ
(C) 容認できる
(D) 容認できる程度に

2. Nakamoto さんは、月曜日に事業担当重役とし
て Hwang 産業社に加わります。

(A) ～に加わる
(B) ～を維持する
(C) ～を取引する
(D) ～を合併させる

3. 当店の方針により、セール商品の価格交渉には応
じかねますのでご了承ください。

(A) 交渉できる
(B) 交渉人
(C) 交渉
(D) 交渉している

4. プレゼンテーションで、Mennon さんはその提案
の長所と短所をざっと説明しました。

(A) ～を含んだ
(B) ～を概説した
(C) 固執した
(D) ～に同行した

5. Dorbush 市議会は、その祖父が市立公園を設計
した Mazzulo さんに市の鍵を贈呈しました。

(A) ～すること
(B) ～である
(C) その人が
(D) その人の

6. Lizor コンサルタント社は、企業合併をうまく取
りまとめることにおいて豊富な経験があります。

(A) わずかに
(B) 一般的に
(C) うまく
(D) もともと

7. 会社の顧客基盤拡大への献身によって、Simon
さんは今年、ボーナスを獲得しました。

(A) ～をささげる［動詞の原形／現在形］
(B) 献身的な
(C) ～をささげる［動詞の三人称単数現在形］
(D) 献身

88

Part 6

問題 8-11 は次の広告に関するものです。

ご家族のお祝いのための魅力的な環境をお探しですか？ 英領ヴァージン諸島の Tortola 島にある美しい Hibiscus Tropical Garden をご検討されてはいかがでしょう？ 50 年にわたって、この場所は熱帯の花々の現役の養苗場でした。そして 15 年前に、敷地と建物が全面的に改修されました。この 100 万ドルの投資の結果が、田園の風情と現代的な設備という唯一無二の組み合わせです。倉庫を改築した当館施設では、最大 250 名のお客さまにご夕食とエンターテインメントをご提供できます。ご夕食が終わったら、当施設の最新音響システムで、お連れさまが一晩じゅう元気にダンスに興じられること請け合いです。

当館の行事予定表は毎シーズンあっという間に埋まります。*ですから、今すぐ特別なイベントの計画を始めましょう。284-555-0012 または ewilder@hibiscustropicalgarden.co.vg の Evan Wilder までご連絡ください。

---

*問題 11 の挿入文の訳

8. (A) 探した
(B) 探すために
(C) 探している
(D) 探す

9. (A) 隔絶された
(B) 改修された
(C) 放棄された
(D) 貸し出された

10. (A) 組み合わせ
(B) 〜を組み合わせるために
(C) 組み合わせ可能な
(D) 〜を組み合わせる

11. (A) 残念ながら、もう花苗は販売していません。
(B) この島には、船と飛行機で行くことができます。
(C) 一番の眺めは島の南端にあります。
(D) ですから、今すぐ特別なイベントの計画を始めましょう。

Part 7

問題 12-14 は次の招待状に関するものです。

勤続のお祝い

Astoria 産業社に
長年勤務してくれた従業員各位の献身的な尽力を共にたたえましょう。

基調講演が最高執行責任者 Henry Wilson によって行われる予定で、
彼は過去 43 年にわたって当社で見てきた変化について語ります。

地元選出の議員の方々と Astoria 産業社の全従業員の皆さまの
ご参加をお待ちしております!

4 月 10 日(水)午前 10:00 ～午前 11:30

さまざまな軽食をご用意しております。

Astoria 産業社 本社
会議室 B
Hoey 通り 29 番地
Kamo、ファンガレイ 0112

12. 4 月 10 日のイベントの目的は何ですか。

    (A) 新しい会社役員を歓迎すること

    (B) 会社の創立記念日を祝うこと

    (C) ある従業員のグループに感謝すること

    (D) 新本社の開業を記念すること

13. Wilson さんについて何が示唆されていますか。

    (A) ファンガレイで選出された議員である。

    (B) Astoria 産業社に数十年間勤務している。

    (C) 自ら進んでこのイベントを企画した。

    (D) 彼の執務室は会議室 B の隣にある。

14. イベントでは何が出されると思われますか。

    (A) 選りすぐった前菜

    (B) 3 品のコース料理

    (C) ビュッフェ形式のランチ

    (D) ケータリングのブランチ

問題 15-19 は次の報告書、E メール、記事に関するものです。

<table>
<tr><td colspan="5" align="center">**Naro ガラス社**
ウェブ・トラフィック解析
作成者：Evan Morin</td></tr>
<tr><th>どのように訪問者が Naro ガラス社を知ったか</th><th>1 月</th><th>2 月</th><th>3 月</th><th>4 月</th></tr>
<tr><td>ウェブアドレスを直接入力</td><td>23,000</td><td>22,000</td><td>20,000</td><td>21,000</td></tr>
<tr><td>インターネットの検索エンジンを利用</td><td>19,000</td><td>20,000</td><td>21,000</td><td>18,000</td></tr>
<tr><td>クライアントのウェブサイトからの参照</td><td>19,000</td><td>19,000</td><td>19,000</td><td>7,000*</td></tr>
<tr><td>ソーシャルメディアサイトのリンクをクリック</td><td>17,000</td><td>16,000</td><td>14,000</td><td>13,000</td></tr>
<tr><td colspan="5">*Lensegent 社（クライアント経由の主な当社参照元）について追って検討のこと</td></tr>
</table>

E メールメッセージ

受信者： Evan Morin
送信者： Rie Kondo
日付： 5 月 1 日
件名： ウェブ・トラフィック

こんにちは、Evan

当 Naro ガラス社ウェブサイトのトラフィック解析表を送ってくださり、ありがとうございます。これは参考になります。数字を回復させるためにできることの 1 つは、Zermavise のようなサイトで存在感を高めることです。そうすれば、この区分のトラフィックを、年初当時のように 17,000 ヒットまで引き上げることができるはずです。また、Lensegent 社でのトラブルがその分野で当社の数字を押し下げているようなので、クライアントサイト一覧を広げることも必要です。

よろしくお願いします。

Rie

デンバー（5月10日）——堅調だった昨年第4四半期の後、Lensegent 社は不安定な新年のスタートを切った。同社 CEO の Sara Ormond が2月に退任となった。その後4月に、同社ウェブサイトは技術的問題で度々障害を起こした。今月に入り、Lensegent 社は海外拡大の計画を一時中止し、国内営業部隊を再編することを発表した。この一連の混乱により、投資家の間に、写真用部材市場のトップ企業である同社が競争力を維持できるのかという疑問が生じている。新 CEO の Maxwell Holland は投資家に対し、低迷は一時的なものであり、彼の再編計画によって Lensegent 社は9月までにより強い企業になるだろうと断言した。

15. Morin さんは誰だと思われますか。

(A) 営業担当者
(B) データアナリスト
(C) 会社の CEO
(D) 人事の専門家

16. いつ最大数の訪問者が検索エンジン経由で Naro ガラス社のウェブサイトを見つけましたか。

(A) 1月
(B) 2月
(C) 3月
(D) 4月

17. Zermavise とは何だと思われますか。

(A) ウェブ上の新聞
(B) インターネットの検索ツール
(C) クライアントのウェブサイト
(D) ソーシャルメディアサイト

18. Lensegent 社から Naro ガラス社への照会が減った原因は何だと思われますか。

(A) Lensegent 社の経営陣の変更
(B) Lensegent 社のウェブサイトに起きたトラブル
(C) Lensegent 社の海外事業部の閉鎖
(D) Lensegent 社の国内営業部隊の再編

19. Lensegent 社は何を作っていますか。

(A) カメラ部品
(B) 眼鏡
(C) 宝飾品
(D) コンピューターソフト

Section

15

正解一覧

Part 5	1 (C)	2 (A)	3 (C)	4 (C)	5 (A)	6 (D)	7 (C)	
Part 6	8 (A)	9 (C)	10 (B)	11 (D)				
Part 7	12 (B)	13 (C)	14 (A)	15 (C)	16 (A)	17 (A)	18 (D)	19 (A)

Part 5

1. Yi さんは、倉庫に保管されている箱を慎重に数えたことを証明して、チェックリストに署名しました。

(A) ほぼ間違いなく
(B) 潜在的に
(C) 慎重に
(D) 広々と

2. 昨日の講習会中に Jodie Guerra はメモを取りましたが、彼女はそれを E メールでグループと共有するつもりです。

(A) そしてそれを
(B) それらを
(C) 他の
(D) 幾つかの

3. 来月、由緒ある Northbridge 図書館の 50 枚以上の窓が交換されます。

(A) 驚嘆した
(B) 一時的な
(C) 歴史的な
(D) 住居用の

4. 上司の許可なく在宅勤務をすることは厳しく禁じられています。

(A) 急いで
(B) 緊張して
(C) 厳しく
(D) しっかりと

5. 写真コンテストの受賞者は、作品が図書館のロビーに展示される予定です。

(A) 展示されて
(B) 展示された
(C) 展示されるために
(D) 展示されてきた

6. Vitas ジムの新しいプールの寸法は 15 メートル × 35 メートルです。

(A) 形
(B) 方向
(C) 位置
(D) 寸法

7. Chan さんは、前四半期の間に彼のチームが販売目標を超えたと述べました。

(A) 〜している間
(B) 〜と同時に
(C) 〜の間に
(D) 近くの

Part 6

問題 8-11 は次の手紙に関するものです。

Ainsworth HVAC：ご自宅のあらゆる快適さのニーズのために。

大切なお客さまへ

ご利用履歴によりますと、お客さまは、暖房・換気・空調（HVAC）の無料の任意検査に使えるキャンペーン資格をまだ使用されないままお持ちです。家庭や職場の非常に多くの責務で頭がいっぱいだと、多くの方にとって、こうした設備や配管にはきちんとした保守と清掃が必要だと覚えておくことは困難です。*半年に 1 度点検を行えば、空気の質を維持するのに役立ちます。ところが、点検を先延ばしにしていると、光熱費の増加や設備の損傷を招く恐れがあります。今すぐ、当社にお電話いただきご予約ください！

敬具

皆さまの Ainsworth HVAC 専門スタッフ一同

---

*問題 10 の挿入文の訳

8. (A) 〜を示す
(B) 〜を示すだろう
(C) 〜を示すための
(D) 〜を示している

9. (A) 〜を管理する
(B) 〜を割り当てる
(C) 〜を覚えている
(D) 〜を依頼する

10. (A) それゆえ、Ainsworth HVAC はあなたのお取引に感謝いたします。
(B) 半年に 1 度点検を行えば、空気の質を維持するのに役立ちます。
(C) 特別なお支払いプランをご用意しています。
(D) 当社のウェブサイトを訪れ、当社がご提供している各サービスをご覧ください。

11. (A) 技術者
(B) 工程
(C) 決断
(D) 設備

Section

16

Part 7

問題 12-14 は次の手紙に関するものです。

Athena Pro Star • Parkwood 通り 575 番地 • コーバリス市、オレゴン州 97330

10 月 14 日

Angelika MacGorain
East College 大通り 214 番地
コーバリス市、オレゴン州　97330

MacGorain 様

Athena Pro Star プラチナ会員権をご購入いただき、ありがとうございます！ これからはお客さまは当施設の最新設備およびエアロビクスと屋内サイクリングのクラスをご利用になれます。また、お持ちのプラチナ会員カードは、Athena Pro Star のいずれのフランチャイズ店舗へのご入店にもご利用いただけます。*これには当社の全海外店舗も含まれます。

10 月 9 日にお支払い済みのお客さまの入会金と月会費の日割分を処理いたしました。今後は毎月 1 日に請求させていただきます。お支払いは直接店舗にて、もしくはウェブサイトから行っていただくことができます。ウェブサイトでのお支払いは、お客さまのアカウントに反映されるまで最低 2 日かかることをご了承ください。

敬具

Tamar Chivadze (署名)
Tamar Chivadze
会員サービス担当

---

*問題 14 の挿入文の訳

12. Athena Pro Star はどんな種類の事業ですか。

(A) 電子機器店

(B) フィットネスクラブ

(C) 職業訓練事業

(D) ホテルチェーン

13. 手紙によると、何月何日に MacGorain さんに次回の請求がされますか。

(A) 10 月 9 日

(B) 10 月 14 日

(C) 11 月 1 日

(D) 11 月 3 日

14. [1]、[2]、[3]、[4] と記載された箇所のうち、次の文が入るのに最もふさわしいのはどれですか。

「これには当社の全海外店舗も含まれます」

(A) [1]

(B) [2]

(C) [3]

(D) [4]

Section

16

問題 15-19 は次の 2 通の E メールと表に関するものです。

送信者：	Jon Cuthbert
受信者：	Farah Moosa
日付：	6 月 16 日
件名：	協議会の公開討論会
添付ファイル：	🔗 パネリスト候補とテーマ

Farah さん

今度のチューリッヒ女性指導力協議会のために、公開討論会の取りまとめをしているところです。登壇者は、自分が選んだキャリア分野での経験について、各自 15 分間の講演を行います。その後、公開討論会の自由討論が始まります。

今のところ、あなたの他に登壇者を 4 人招待することを検討しています。それぞれの方にお話しいただくテーマも付記して、これらのパネリスト候補のお名前を添付しましたので、ご確認ください。Lordachescu 博士はあなたの同僚だと理解しております。もし可能であれば、あなたの講演内容や討論に対する発言が博士のものと十分異なるようにしていただけないでしょうか。

ところで、追加のパネリストの方々について、あなたご自身の提案を聞かせていただけませんか。協議会の開幕は 8 月中旬で、こうした公開討論会の手配は 7 月下旬までに最終決定する必要がありますので、この件について近日中にご返信ください。

よろしくお願いします。

Jon

提案されたテーマとパネリスト

パネリスト	経歴	テーマ
Karine Bastin	全国的なベーカリーチェーンの創業者	小規模ビジネスにおける女性たち
Cici Lordachescu	大学の人文学部長	学術界の女性たち
Alicia Ward	自己啓発の講演者	フリーランスで働く女性たち
Daniela von Theumer	女子プロバレーボール監督	スポーツ界の女性たち

送信者：	Farah Moosa
受信者：	Jon Cuthbert
日付：	6月17日
件名：	協議会の公開討論会

こんにちは、Jon

あなたが作成した公開討論会プランは良さそうに思えます。ただ、私は von Theumer さんのテーマについて懸念しています。というのは、他のテーマとの関連性が薄いように思うからです。代わりに、彼女自身や彼女のチームメンバーの多くが有名であることから、「脚光を浴びる女性たち」について、もっと一般的な話をしてもらうことはできないでしょうか。

追加のパネリスト1、2名の案をすぐに折り返しご連絡します。また、確定したパネリストの方々には、当方の宣伝資料に掲載できるように、経歴詳細を送ってもらうよう依頼していただけますか。

どうぞよろしくお願いします。

Farah

15. 1通目の E メールによると、協議会はいつ開催されますか。

(A) 6月
(B) 7月
(C) 8月
(D) 9月

16. Moosa さんについて何が示唆されていますか。

(A) 大学に勤めている。
(B) これまで Cuthbert さんに会ったことがない。
(C) スポーツをしない。
(D) 世界中の協議会で講演している。

17. 表によると、誰が自分で事業を立ち上げ、それを拡大しましたか。

(A) Bastin さん
(B) Lordachescu 博士
(C) Ward さん
(D) von Theumer さん

18. 協議会のどの討論会のテーマが変更されると思われますか。

(A) 小規模ビジネスにおける女性たち
(B) 学術界の女性たち
(C) フリーランスで働く女性たち
(D) スポーツ界の女性たち

19. 2通目の E メールで Moosa さんは何を依頼していますか。

(A) 登壇者が自身に関する情報を提供すること
(B) パネリストの一覧に自分を加えること
(C) Cuthbert さんが幾つかの宣伝資料を見直すこと
(D) 協議会の場で書籍を購入できるようにすること

正解一覧

Part 5	1 (C)	2 (A)	3 (C)	4 (A)	5 (B)	6 (A)	7 (B)
Part 6	8 (D)	9 (A)	10 (A)	11 (C)			
Part 7	12 (B)	13 (A)	14 (A)	15 (C)	16 (C)	17 (A)	18 (C)

	19 (B)	20 (A)

Part 5

1. Vannuck のジムバッグは標準的なロッカーに簡単に収まるように設計されています。

(A) 最も簡単な
(B) より簡単な
(C) 簡単に
(D) 簡単さ

2. 保守チームはドアの取り付けを完了するために明日また来る予定です。

(A) 〜を完了する
(B) 〜を決定する
(C) 〜を継承する
(D) 説明する

3. ほとんどの滞在客が、Jodi's Haven ホテルの最もお気に入りの特長は専用ビーチだと言っています。

(A) 親切な行為
(B) 好意的な
(C) 最もお気に入りの
(D) 好意的に

4. 今夜のコンサートから得た収益の一部は慈善事業に寄付されます。

(A) 〜から
(B) 〜の
(C) 〜と共に
(D) 上へ

5. Dainville コミュニケーションズ社は、来年収入が倍増すると見込まれています。

(A) 〜を見込む
(B) 見込まれた
(C) 期待して
(D) 期待

6. 昨年の改装の結果、科学博物館の部屋は配置が変わりました。

(A) 再配置された
(B) 再配置している
(C) 〜を再配置する [動詞の三人称単数現在形]
(D) 〜を再配置する [動詞の原形／現在形]

7. 情報技術はますます、子どもが何でどのように遊ぶかを決定付けるようになっています。

(A) 連続して
(B) ますます
(C) 深く
(D) 非常に

Part 6

問題 8-11 は次の E メールに関するものです。

送信者：顧客部 <accounts@binghamhomerentals.co.uk>
受信者：Jensen Cooper <jcooper@msqmail.co.uk>
日付：4 月 30 日
件名：貸別荘のお支払いについて（#1452）

来たる休日のために Pierce Lake 1452 番地の当社コテージを賃借いただき、ありがとうございます。賃借料のお支払いが現時点で 2 日遅れておりますことをお知らせいたします。ご予約が取り消されないようにするには、本日の営業時間終了時までにお支払いください。*お支払いは、ウェブサイトおよびお電話のどちらからでも承っております。

お支払いをうっかり失念するのは非常によくあることだと、当社は十分理解しております。それでもなお、今後 2 日以内にお支払いがない場合、当社はご予約をキャンセルせざるを得ず、また、お預かり金も返金いたしかねます。

よろしくお願いいたします。

Bill Bellows
Bingham レンタル別荘社

---

*問題 10 の挿入文の訳

8. (A) 最新の
(B) 遅れること
(C) 後で
(D) 遅れて

9. (A) 予約
(B) 許可
(C) 広告
(D) 辛抱

10. (A) お支払いは、ウェブサイトおよびお電話のどちらからでも承っております。
(B) 湖畔の別荘は 6 月から 8 月まで週単位での賃貸に対応可能です。
(C) お客さまの家屋を他人に賃貸できるようにするには補修が必要かもしれません。
(D) 私たちは毎年、数百人のお客さまとお取引をしております。

11. (A) 〜を預けた
(B) 〜を預けている
(C) 預かり金
(D) 預金者

Part 7

問題 12-15 は次の E メールに関するものです。

受信者:	Barnsley 研究所の全職員
送信者:	Shawn Casper
日付:	8月3日
件名:	工事承認

職員各位

Barnsley 研究所の窓交換の要望が本社から承認されました。Barnsley 研究所は築 40 年以上で、Solution ファイバーワイヤー社のさまざまな施設の中でも最も古いものです。この研究所には、建設当初の窓がまだ残っているため、その交換は快適さおよび節電効果を大いに向上させるでしょう。

請負業者は今週土曜日に建物の東側から開始して、週末のうちに作業を終える予定です。金曜日に、全ての家具やパソコン類や同様の品々は、新しい窓の設置工事中に損傷を受けないよう、東側の各オフィスから運び出されなければなりません。引っ越し専門業者がこれらの物を一時保管のための所定の場所へ運んでくれる契約になっています。影響を受ける従業員は木曜日に全ての私物を持ち帰り、金曜日は在宅で勤務する用意をしておくことをお勧めします。建物の東側で勤務していない職員は、通常通りオフィスに出勤してください。

続く 3 度の週末にわたって、作業はそれぞれ、建物の西側、南側、北側と移っていきます。この過程の中で不明な点が生じた場合は、私に直接ご連絡ください。

敬具

Shawn Casper
Barnsley 研究所　建物管理責任者
Solution ファイバーワイヤー社

12. Solution ファイバーワイヤー社について何が示されていますか。

    (A) 施設を拡張する必要がある。

    (B) 複数の場所に職員がいる。

    (C) 最近、他社に買収された。

    (D) 最近、本社が移転した。

13. Casper さんは、工事完了の結果どうなると言っていますか。

    (A) エネルギー費用が下がる

    (B) 職場がもっと静かになる

    (C) スペースをもっと効率的に使えるようになる

    (D) 外観がより現代的になる

14. 一部の職員は何をする用意をしておくべきですか。

    (A) 在宅で勤務する

    (B) 新しいオフィスを選ぶ

    (C) 自身の家具を動かす

    (D) 保管場所を特定する

15. 工事はどこで終わりますか。

    (A) 東側

    (B) 西側

    (C) 北側

    (D) 南側

問題 16-20 は次の E メール、ウェブページ、記事に関するものです。

受信者：	Todd Roe
送信者：	Erma Yee
日付：	2 月 12 日　木曜日
件名：	プリンター

Todd さん

私たちがもうすぐ設立する会社のために購入すべきプリンターについて、私の意見をお伝えします。思い出していただけるでしょうが、私たちは大きな仕事をぼうっと待ってはいられないということになりました。最初は小さな注文──その注文しかなければシャツたった 1 枚でも──を受けることになるので、私たちには高価過ぎないプリンターが必要です。また毎年数回の展示会を予定しているため、あちこちに楽に持ち運べるものが必要になります。Productreviews.com には、私たちが選択するのに役立つ情報があるはずです。そのサイトをチェックして、どのプリンターを買うべきか私に推薦してください。

よろしくお願いします。

Erma

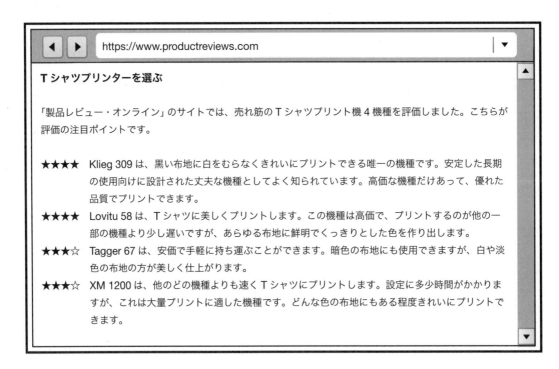

https://www.productreviews.com

T シャツプリンターを選ぶ

「製品レビュー・オンライン」のサイトでは、売れ筋の T シャツプリント機 4 機種を評価しました。こちらが評価の注目ポイントです。

★★★★　Klieg 309 は、黒い布地に白をむらなくきれいにプリントできる唯一の機種です。安定した長期の使用向けに設計された丈夫な機種としてよく知られています。高価な機種だけあって、優れた品質でプリントできます。

★★★★　Lovitu 58 は、T シャツに美しくプリントします。この機種は高価で、プリントするのが他の一部の機種より少し遅いですが、あらゆる布地に鮮明でくっきりとした色を作り出します。

★★★☆　Tagger 67 は、安価で手軽に持ち運ぶことができます。暗色の布地にも使用できますが、白や淡色の布地の方が美しく仕上がります。

★★★☆　XM 1200 は、他のどの機種よりも速く T シャツにプリントします。設定に多少時間がかかりますが、これは大量プリントに適した機種です。どんな色の布地にもある程度きれいにプリントできます。

T シャツの大規模ビジネス

Marcus Schreiner 記

9 月 25 日――オンラインビジネス市場における進展を観察している人であれば、あるトレンドに気付くことだろう。アパレルプリント企業数の急増だ。こうした企業は、後に衣類や服飾品にプリントされることになるデザインの考案および提出を一般人から募る。デザインはその後、その企業のウェブサイト上に掲載され、消費者はそこでお目当てのデザインを注文できる。デザインの考案者は利益の一定割合を受け取る。

企業の中には、Kimmytee 社のように、最低 100 枚の注文がないとプリントサービスを行わないところもある。Faymoor 衣料社のように、顧客と話し合って最低発注数を 12 点という少数にしている企業もある。さらにまた、それぞれ創業 6 カ月と創業 10 年の Akahi シャツ社と Temizo プリント社のように、最低発注数をいっさい求めない企業もある。

16. Klieg 309 について何が示されていますか。

(A) 市場で最も人気のある機種である。
(B) 競合機種より長い間市場で販売されている。
(C) 信頼性が高いという評判がある。
(D) 操作しやすいことで知られている。

17. ウェブページで述べられている全ての機種に共通することは何ですか。

(A) 暗色の布地にプリントできる。
(B) 軽量である。
(C) 平均より速い。
(D) 比較的安価である。

18. Roe さんは Yee さんにどのプリンターを薦めたと思われますか。

(A) The Klieg 309
(B) The Lovitu 58
(C) The Tagger 67
(D) The XM 1200

19. 記事の第 1 段落 1 行目にある "monitor" に最も意味が近いのは

(A) ～を信じる
(B) ～を見守る
(C) ～を監督する
(D) ～に頼る

20. Yee さんと Roe さんは、記事で述べられているどの会社で働いていると思われますか。

(A) Akahi シャツ社
(B) Faymoor 衣料社
(C) Kimmytee 社
(D) Temizo プリント社

正解一覧

Part 5	1 (C)	2 (D)	3 (B)	4 (A)	5 (A)	6 (B)	7 (B)		
Part 6	8 (C)	9 (D)	10 (D)	11 (A)					
Part 7	12 (B)	13 (D)	14 (B)	15 (C)	16 (A)	17 (B)	18 (A)	19 (B)	20 (C)

Part 5

1. Byun さんのオフィスは塗装中なので、彼女は一時的に 212 号室で働く予定です。

(A) 堅く
(B) 広く
(C) 一時的に
(D) 構造的に

2. 従業員の業績評価会議は会議室で行われる予定です。

(A) 関係がある
(B) 言われて
(C) 適用されて
(D) 開催されて

3. Ober 社の取締役会は、新社長選出後、再び会合を持ちます。

(A) 〜を選ぶ［動詞の原形／現在形］
(B) 選挙
(C) 選挙の
(D) 〜を選ぶ［動詞の三人称単数現在形］

4. 翻訳者の仕事の機会は今後 10 年間に増加すると予測されています。

(A) 次の
(B) 真っすぐな
(C) 追加の
(D) 生産的な

5. 公演が始まったら、全ての携帯電話は音が出ないようにしてください。

(A) 始まる
(B) 始まるだろう
(C) 始まろうとしていた
(D) 始まった

6. 私たちの顧客には、投資に対して積極的なアプローチを好む方もいれば、慎重な方もいます。

(A) 〜にもかかわらず
(B) ところが一方
(C) だから
(D) なぜなら

7. 作家であり、熟達の芸術家でもある Jo Ng さんが、月曜日に図書館で自身の最新刊にサインをします。

(A) 〜を成し遂げている
(B) 熟達した
(C) 業績
(D) 〜を成し遂げる

Part 6

問題 8-11 は次のお知らせに関するものです。

Kurlinkus 種子社社員各位へのお知らせ

今月、何人かのお客さまから注文に関する問題が報告されています。具体的には、お客さま方は種子の入っていない袋を受け取っています。今後、配送する前に必ず一つ一つの袋を点検してください。当社はこれ以上、空の袋を誤って出荷したくありません。当社の急成長に伴って、既存業務に負担がかかっているのは分かっています。*今回の問題がその明白な証拠です。経営陣は現在、どうすれば当社の高い品質基準を維持しつつ高まる需要にもっとうまく対応できるかを見極めようと、当社の作業工程の評価をしています。それまでの間、種子を包装する際は、特別入念に行ってください。

よろしくお願いします。

Kurlinkus 種子社経営陣

---

*問題 10 の挿入文の訳

8.
(A) それゆえ
(B) そこでまた
(C) 具体的には
(D) それにもかかわらず

9.
(A) 古い
(B) 濡れた
(C) 汚れた
(D) 空の

10.
(A) 私は検査報告書を受け取りました。
(B) 明日から作業を再開して結構です。
(C) それらはもう出荷の準備ができています。
(D) 今回の問題がその明白な証拠です。

11.
(A) 〜を包装している
(B) 一袋の〜
(C) 彼らは〜を包装する
(D) 〜を包装してしまって

Part 7

問題 12-15 は次のオンラインチャットでの話し合いに関するものです。

Shanice Rowe（午前 10 時 12 分）いいニュースです、Minseo と Ademar。Perkins さんと話したところ、Zeno セメント社のプロジェクトに関する提案書の作成を私たちに進めてほしいそうです。

Minseo Jeong（午前 10 時 12 分）えっ、もう彼に話したのですか。

Shanice Rowe（午前 10 時 13 分）はい、ちょっと雑談をしました。彼は私たちのアイデアは進める価値があると考えています。今日、彼が月曜朝の定例会議から出て来たところでばったり会いました。

Ademar Souza（午前 10 時 14 分）それは素晴らしい。それで、皆が空いているのはいつですか。私は、今週は火曜日か木曜日の午後 3 時以降なら集まれます——あるいは金曜日ならいつでも。

Minseo Jeong（午前 10 時 15 分）その通りです、Ademar。Zeno セメント社の件を進めるには Perkins さんの力添えがぜひとも必要です。

Shanice Rowe（午前 10 時 15 分）私は明日の午後遅くが空いていて、あるいは木曜日の午後 3 時半か金曜日の午後 2 時半でも集まれます。

Minseo Jeong（午前 10 時 16 分）週のもっと早くに集まるようにできませんか。私は火曜日の午後がいいのですが、もしお二人が大丈夫なら。

Ademar Souza（午前 10 時 17 分）私は構いませんよ。

Shanice Rowe（午前 10 時 17 分）明日の午後 4 時はどうですか。

Minseo Jeong（午前 10 時 18 分）いいですね。Albright 会議室で集まりましょう。1 時間の予約を入れておきます。それでいいですか。

Ademar Souza（午前 10 時 19 分）ありがたいです。では、打ち合わせの間にまとめられるように、全員が自分なりの大まかな草案を持ち寄りましょう。

12. Perkins さんについて何が示されていますか。

    (A) セメント製品を専門としている。

    (B) 毎週月曜日に会議に参加する。

    (C) Rowe さんと同じ仕事をしている。

    (D) 会社の創業者である。

13. 午前 10 時 14 分に、Souza さんは "That's wonderful" という発言で、何を意味していると思われますか。

    (A) Zeno セメント社のプロジェクトがまとまって驚いている。

    (B) Perkins さんが追加スタッフの雇用に同意してくれて喜んでいる。

    (C) Zeno セメント社との合併が進むことに満足している。

    (D) Perkins さんがある仕事を承認してくれてうれしい。

14. 書き手たちはいつ集まって仕事を進めますか。

    (A) 月曜日の午後 3 時

    (B) 火曜日の午後 4 時

    (C) 木曜日の午後 3 時 30 分

    (D) 金曜日の午後 2 時 30 分

15. 次に何が起こると思われますか。

    (A) Rowe さんがプレゼンテーションを行う。

    (B) Perkins さんが提案書を吟味する。

    (C) Jeong さんが部屋を予約する。

    (D) Souza さんが Zeno セメント社に連絡を取る。

問題 16-20 は次のウェブサイトとお知らせに関するものです。

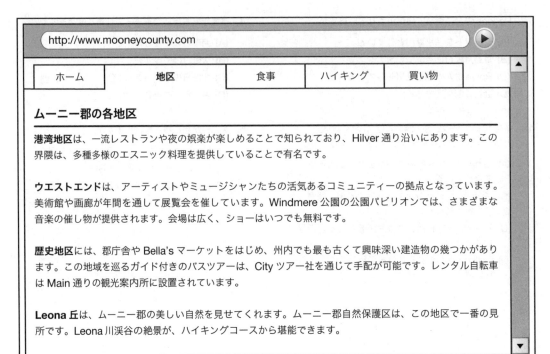

http://www.mooneycounty.com

| ホーム | 地区 | 食事 | ハイキング | 買い物 |

ムーニー郡の各地区

港湾地区は、一流レストランや夜の娯楽が楽しめることで知られており、Hilver 通り沿いにあります。この界隈は、多種多様のエスニック料理を提供していることで有名です。

ウエストエンドは、アーティストやミュージシャンたちの活気あるコミュニティーの拠点となっています。美術館や画廊が年間を通して展覧会を催しています。Windmere 公園の公園パビリオンでは、さまざまな音楽の催し物が提供されます。会場は広く、ショーはいつでも無料です。

歴史地区には、郡庁舎や Bella's マーケットをはじめ、州内でも最も古くて興味深い建造物の幾つかがあります。この地域を巡るガイド付きのバスツアーは、City ツアー社を通じて手配が可能です。レンタル自転車は Main 通りの観光案内所に設置されています。

Leona 丘は、ムーニー郡の美しい自然を見せてくれます。ムーニー郡自然保護区は、この地区で一番の見所です。Leona 川渓谷の絶景が、ハイキングコースから堪能できます。

お知らせ：ムーニー郡パレード

この毎年恒例の人気イベントが、今度の土曜日、正午に郡庁舎前出発で開催されます。例年通り、パレード隊は Keel 通りを行進して、Laurel 道に入ります。終点は Windmere 公園です。パレード終了後は、Santiago Heart バンドが午後 2 時より公園パビリオンで演奏する予定です。また、パレードのさまざまな部門での上位入賞者を表彰して賞が授与されます。

パレード経路付近では道路が一時通行止めになるため車両は迂回する必要があること、また路上駐車も極めて制限されることを郡当局より市民の皆さまへいま一度お知らせします。ご見物の皆さまはシャトルバスをご利用くださるようお願いします。バスは午前 10 時 30 分から 20 分おきに終日運行します。

16. このウェブサイトは誰に向けられたものだと思われますか。

(A) ムーニー郡への観光客

(B) 不動産開発業者

(C) パレード参加者

(D) 行政府職員

17. ウェブサイトによると、港湾地区で提供されるものは何ですか。

(A) ガイド付きのバスツアー

(B) さまざまな食事の選択肢

(C) 眺めのよい遊歩道

(D) 注目すべき建築物がある場所

18. 歴史地区について示唆されていないことは何ですか。

(A) 歴史博物館がある。

(B) サイクリングに向いている。

(C) パレードが毎年そこから出発する。

(D) そこでバスツアーが提供されている。

19. パレード後の音楽演奏について何が示されていますか。

(A) 才能のある地元ミュージシャンたちを紹介する。

(B) 無料で一般公開される。

(C) Leona 丘で行われる。

(D) 受賞歴のあるバンドを呼び物にしている。

20. お知らせではどんな勧告がなされていますか。

(A) Windmere 公園の工事中の場所を避ける

(B) パレードの最高の眺めを得るには Laurel 道沿いを行く

(C) 交通量をできる限り減らすために公共交通機関を利用する

(D) マーケットを訪れるために早い時間に着く

Section 19 正解／訳

正解一覧

Part 5	**1** (C)	**2** (A)	**3** (C)	**4** (D)	**5** (A)	**6** (C)	**7** (A)	
Part 6	**8** (C)	**9** (A)	**10** (C)	**11** (B)				
Part 7	**12** (B)	**13** (B)	**14** (A)	**15** (B)	**16** (C)	**17** (A)	**18** (A)	**19** (B)

Part 5

1. 全ての従業員は、休暇に出かける前に共用冷蔵庫から自分の食品を取り出さなければなりません。

(A) 〜の間に
(B) 〜の上へ
(C) 〜の前に
(D) 〜を除いて

2. 西アフリカから商品を輸入することで、Asante 衣料品社は業界での強固な地位を獲得してきました。

(A) 産業
(B) 産業の
(C) 〜を産業化する
(D) 〜を産業化している

3. 今月、Thunderbolt 食品社は新しい設備を収容するために製造エリアを拡張する予定です。

(A) 〜を想像する
(B) 〜を持ってくる
(C) 〜を拡張する
(D) 〜の利益になる

4. Fandango 社の営業チームは、自社のサービスをより効果的に売り込むための戦略を練っています。

(A) 効果［名詞の単数形］
(B) 効果［名詞の複数形］
(C) 効果的な
(D) 効果的に

5. Aiduk 電子機器社のリサイクルの新たな取り組みは、毎月生じる廃棄物の量を大幅に減らすことになるでしょう。

(A) 新構想
(B) 目的
(C) 印象
(D) 下見

6. 輸送中に破損したご注文品は商品のご返品後、直ちに交換いたします。

(A) 〜する場所で
(B) 〜を越えて
(C) 〜の後で
(D) 〜まで

7. 競合他社は行っていませんが、Ensin 社は全ての製品を消費者に直接配送しています。

(A) 〜ではあるが
(B) 〜は別として
(C) 〜と同様に
(D) 特に

112

Part 6

問題 8-11 は次の報道発表に関するものです。

地方独立食料雑貨店協会（PIGA）は本日、Edo Dorr が同協会の理事長兼 CEO に選任されたことを発表しました。Dorr 氏は以前、同協会の事業担当副理事長を務めていました。Dorr 氏は理事長として、独立食料雑貨店の社会的認知の向上に重点的に取り組む予定です。

「買い物客は巨大スーパーチェーンに替わるものを求めています」と PIGA の広報担当 Christine Franco は語りました。「今こそ、買い物客を再び引きつけるような便利さときめ細かなサービスへと回帰すべき時です。*それがまさに PIGA の食料雑貨店が提供するものです。私たちは、Edo Dorr がこの協会を未来へ導いてくれる適任者であると確信しています」。

---

*問題 11 の挿入文の訳

8. (A) 代わりに
　　　(B) 同様に
　　　(C) 以前は
　　　(D) 残念ながら

9. (A) 重点的に取り組む予定だ
　　　(B) 重点的に取り組んでいた
　　　(C) 重点的に取り組んでいるところだった
　　　(D) 重点的に取り組んでいただろうに

10. (A) 農業従事者
　　　　(B) 興行主
　　　　(C) 買い物客
　　　　(D) 重役

11. (A) Dorr 氏は余暇に読書を楽しみます。
　　　　(B) それがまさに PIGA の食料雑貨店が提供するものです。
　　　　(C) ショッピングカートは駐車場から撤去されるべきではありません。
　　　　(D) 近年、主要商品の値段が下がっています。

Part 7

問題 12-14 は次の E メールに関するものです。

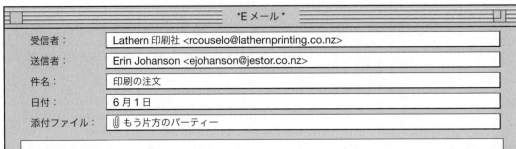

受信者：	Lathern 印刷社 <rcouselo@lathernprinting.co.nz>
送信者：	Erin Johanson <ejohanson@jestor.co.nz>
件名：	印刷の注文
日付：	6 月 1 日
添付ファイル：	📎 もう片方のパーティー

こんにちは、Couselo さん

Erin Johanson です。先ほど電話でお話ししました。このメールに添付されているのが、私が言った電子化した写真です。35 年前の映画のポスターのものです。父はその経歴の中で多数の映画を監督してきましたが、『もう片方のパーティー』は父が最初に制作した作品でした。誕生日プレゼントとして、父のためにこの画像を引き伸ばしていただきたいのです。

可能であれば、69 センチ×104 センチ寸法のポスター用台紙に画像を拡大して印刷していただけますか。そうすれば、オリジナルの大きさを再現できます。添付したものが小さ過ぎてくっきりと印刷できない場合は、お知らせください。父の書庫からもっと鮮明な画像を見つけるようにします。ご遠慮なく 0 3634 443 までお電話ください。また、この依頼を進めてくださる前に費用見積もりを送っていただけますか。

よろしくお願いいたします。

Erin Johanson

12. Couselo さんは誰だと思われますか。

    (A) 元映画監督

    (B) Lathern 印刷社の技術者

    (C) Johanson さんの友人

    (D) 映画会社の従業員

13. E メールと一緒に何が送られていますか。

    (A) プロジェクトの予算書

    (B) ポスターの画像

    (C) 有名な文書

    (D) パーティーの招待状

14. ポスター用台紙の寸法について何が示されていますか。

    (A) ある品物の元のサイズを表している。

    (B) 規格外の寸法である。

    (C) 制作に余分な費用がかかる。

    (D) 前のやりとりに対する訂正である。

Section
19

問題 15-19 は次のフォーム、E メール、手紙に関するものです。

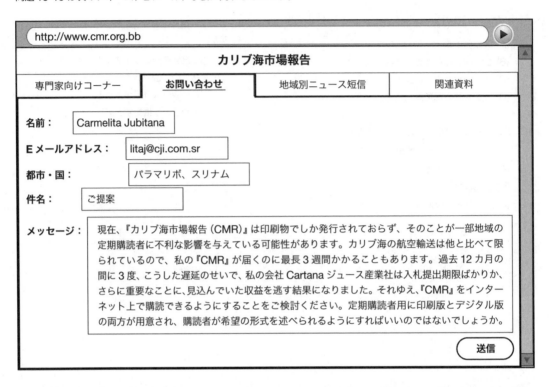

http://www.cmr.org.bb

カリブ海市場報告

| 専門家向けコーナー | **お問い合わせ** | 地域別ニュース短信 | 関連資料 |

名前：   Carmelita Jubitana

E メールアドレス：   litaj@cji.com.sr

都市・国：   パラマリボ、スリナム

件名：   ご提案

メッセージ：   現在、『カリブ海市場報告 (CMR)』は印刷物でしか発行されておらず、そのことが一部地域の定期購読者に不利な影響を与えている可能性があります。カリブ海の航空輸送は他と比べて限られているので、私の『CMR』が届くのに最長 3 週間かかることもあります。過去 12 カ月の間に 3 度、こうした遅延のせいで、私の会社 Cartana ジュース産業社は入札提出期限ばかりか、さらに重要なことに、見込んでいた収益を逃す結果になりました。それゆえ、『CMR』をインターネット上で購読できるようにすることをご検討ください。定期購読者用に印刷版とデジタル版の両方が用意され、購読者が希望の形式を述べられるようにすればいいのではないでしょうか。

送信

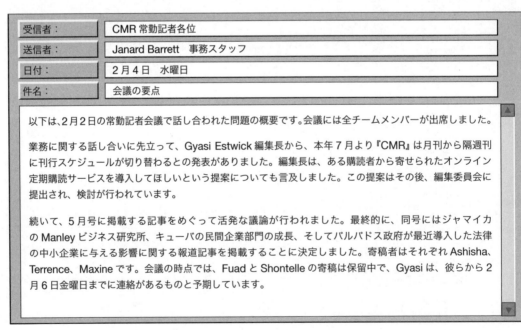

受信者：	CMR 常勤記者各位
送信者：	Janard Barrett　事務スタッフ
日付：	2 月 4 日　水曜日
件名：	会議の要点

以下は、2 月 2 日の常勤記者会議で話し合われた問題の概要です。会議には全チームメンバーが出席しました。

業務に関する話し合いに先立って、Gyasi Estwick 編集長から、本年 7 月より『CMR』は月刊から隔週刊に刊行スケジュールが切り替わるとの発表がありました。編集長は、ある購読者から寄せられたオンライン定期購読サービスを導入してほしいという提案についても言及しました。この提案はその後、編集委員会に提出され、検討が行われています。

続いて、5 月号に掲載する記事をめぐって活発な議論が行われました。最終的に、同号にはジャマイカの Manley ビジネス研究所、キューバの民間企業部門の成長、そしてバルバドス政府が最近導入した法律の中小企業に与える影響に関する報道記事を掲載することに決定しました。寄稿者はそれぞれ Ashisha、Terrence、Maxine です。会議の時点では、Fuad と Shontelle の寄稿は保留中で、Gyasi は、彼らから 2 月 6 日金曜日までに連絡があるものと予期しています。

『カリブ海市場報告』
10月・5巻・第10号

編集長より

今号より、定期購読者の皆さまには、当誌の冊子か電子版のいずれかをご選択いただけるようになりました（詳細は 10 ページをご覧ください）。11 月には、インターネット上で毎週一般向けに放送される番組『論点』がスタートします。この番組は、カリブ海地域における商業や貿易に影響を及ぼす問題や出来事について、地域の財界リーダーたちにインタビューするものです。また、来年 1 月から、『CMR』の冊子版、デジタル版ともに月刊ではなく隔週刊で刊行されます。皆さまがこうした提供物を気に入ってくださることを願っております。

Gyasi Estwick

---

15. Jubitana さんについて正しいことは何ですか。

(A) 彼女の製品はジャマイカだけで売られている。

(B) 彼女の提案は実行された。

(C) 『CMR』のインタビューに応じる予定である。

(D) 1 年以上前に『CMR』の定期購読者になった。

16. 誰が政府規制について論じることになりますか。

(A) Ashisha

(B) Gyasi

(C) Maxine

(D) Terrence

17. Fuad について何が示唆されていますか。

(A) 2 月 2 日の会議に間に合うように記事を提出しなかった。

(B) 2 月に常勤記者チームに加わった。

(C) ミーティングに遅れて出席した。

(D) Shontelle と共同で記事を書く予定である。

18. 『カリブ海市場報告』について何が示されていますか。

(A) 刊行スケジュールの変更が遅れた。

(B) 定期購読者数は近年増加している。

(C) Cartana ジュース産業社が出資している。

(D) 10 ページで構成されている。

19. 『論点』という番組について何が述べられていますか。

(A) 数カ国語で収録される。

(B) 11 月に初めて放送される。

(C) 各回が月に 1 回放送される。

(D) 視聴は『CMR』の定期購読者に限られている。

正解一覧

Part 5	1 (D)	2 (D)	3 (D)	4 (D)	5 (C)	6 (D)	7 (B)		
Part 6	8 (C)	9 (A)	10 (B)	11 (D)					
Part 7	12 (C)	13 (D)	14 (D)	15 (C)	16 (B)	17 (B)	18 (C)	19 (D)	20 (A)

Part 5

1. Banley ホテルでは、宿泊客に周辺地域を巡るガイド付きツアーを提供しています。

(A) 感動した
(B) 集められた
(C) 分けられた
(D) ガイド付きの

2. Alika 自動車販売社は、7 月に最も多数の車を売ったことで Kamaka さんに月間優秀社員賞を授与しました。

(A) 授与された
(B) 〜を授与するための
(C) 〜を授与している
(D) 賞

3. Subline Products 社は地元業者との熾烈な競争にもかかわらず、今月、同社の金属製品の記録的な売り上げを誇りました。

(A) 激しく
(B) 激しさ
(C) 最も激しく
(D) 激しい

4. 手作り家具の需要が高いため、Dana 特注家具社は 3 軒の新展示場を開設しました。

(A) いまや〜なので
(B) 〜という条件で
(C) 〜だが一方
(D) 〜のために

5. Snedeker さんは重役への昇進以前と以後のどちらにおいても、統率力を発揮しました。

(A) どちらか一方の
(B) それらの
(C) 両方とも
(D) 多くの

6. 近代的な道路の急拡大は、小さな町が以前には考えられなかったような規模に成長することに寄与しました。

(A) 穏やかに
(B) 熱心に
(C) 最終的に
(D) 以前は

7. 歴史学者たちは、郡で最も古い木が誰の敷地に生えているかを特定するために昔の地図を調べました。

(A) その
(B) 誰の
(C) 私たちの
(D) 彼らの

Part 6

問題 8-11 は次の記事に関するものです。

ウェリントン（4 月 5 日）――風力タービンエネルギーシステムの大手メーカーSynuor 電力社は本日、同社の
Z762 タービンがこのほど、最新の業界標準規格に完全に適合したことを発表した。この規格は国の電力供給網の
継続的な信頼性を確保するために改正されたものだ。Synuor 社で最も人気のモデルである Z762 は、この規格に
適合するよう改良された。

「非常に多くの新技術がタービンによって利用されているので、こうした規定の変更は不可避でした」と Synuor
電力社の広報担当者 Don Bok は話す。「私たちは電気を供給し続けなければなりません。一時的な供給停止であっ
ても許されません。商取引や日常生活に大きな混乱をもたらしかねないからです。*当社は電力供給の中断を防ぐ
ために自社の務めをぜひとも果たしたいと思っています」。

*問題 11 の挿入文の訳

8. (A) 信頼性が続いている
    (B) それは継続的に信頼できる
    (C) 継続的な信頼性
    (D) 信頼できる状態を継続すること

9. (A) 修正された
    (B) 取り消された
    (C) 疑われた
    (D) 購入された

10. (A) 増加
    (B) 供給停止
    (C) 解決策
    (D) 処理工程

11. (A) 当社は別の規格を提案していました。
    (B) 当社は業界が別の方針を検討してくれること
       を望みます。
    (C) 当社は 30 年以上にわたって風力タービンを
       製造してきました。
    (D) 当社は電力供給の中断を防ぐために自社の務
       めをぜひとも果たしたいと思っています。

Part 7

問題 12-15 は次の E メールに関するものです。

======================= *E メール* =======================	
受信者：	Renata Lehmann; Tomas Cordeiro
送信者：	Stella Dupras
日付：	2 月 20 日
件名：	リサーチ

お疲れさまです、Renata と Tomas。

広告効果の測定を専門にしている会社について、最初のリサーチをしました。2 社の市場調査会社が傑出していました。下に簡単な概要を書いておきますが、3 人で集まって CRX3 ミキサー発売に向けた次の手順について話し合って計画を練った方がいいと思います。

業界最大手の Adeline リサーチグループ（ARG）は数十年の実績があります。ARG は、郵送やオンラインの大規模な調査を活用してデータを収集しています。定量的視点を重視し、広告が対象集団にとってどれくらいの意味があったか、広告が消費者行動にどれくらいの影響を及ぼしたかを評価します。

Clarity トレンド社（CTC）は、別の手法を使うもっと新しい企業です。CTC は、広告が打たれてからの有効性だけを重視するのではなく、制作段階中の検査を取り入れています。初期段階と後期段階における検査を行うのに主にフォーカスグループや小規模な電話調査に依拠しています。

CTC の料金が ARG よりもわずかに高いです。とはいえ、後期段階での変更によって元々の CRX2 ミキサーのキャンペーン活動経費は著しくかさみました。つまり、早いうちから検査をしていたら、あの経費の一部は抑えられていたはずです。私は、これが当社にとって実行性のあるやり方かどうかを見極めるために、CTC に連絡を取ってみたい気持ちになっています。

Stella

12. なぜDuprasさんはこのEメールを書きましたか。

(A) 同僚に締め切りを知らせるため

(B) 商品開発の最新情報を求めるため

(C) 委託業者候補に関する情報を共有するため

(D) 新たな広告キャンペーンについて説明するため

13. 第1段落2行目にある "quick" に最も意味が近いのは

(A) 迅速な

(B) 感動的な

(C) 気の利いた

(D) 手短な

14. CTC について何が示唆されていますか。

(A) CRX2 の広告を制作した。

(B) ARG と同じ手法を使っている。

(C) 小型電化製品を製造している。

(D) ARG の後に設立された。

15. Dupras さんは次に何をすると思われますか。

(A) 値引き交渉をする

(B) 既存の製品を再検査する

(C) さらなる情報を入手する

(D) 提案書を準備する

問題 16-20 は次の 2 通の E メールと予定表に関するものです。

送信者：	Alton Gilman
受信者：	Myeong Kwan
日付：	7 月 21 日
件名：	追ってのご連絡

Kwan 様

先日の春の世界パイプライン協議会でのあなたの会の後で、御社 Krestarr グループに当 DQR 社のエンジニアチーム向けの研修会を企画していただくことについて手短にお話ししました。私たちは会の候補 2 つについてお話ししていました。1 つはパイプライン技術者のための土地利用に関する規制について、もう 1 つはパイプラインが環境に与える影響についてです。秋の協議会であなたがアルバータ州にいらっしゃる際に、ぜひこれを実現させたいと思っています。

Krestarr グループのウェブサイトでは、御社のコンサルティング料は、参加者 10 人までの会が 500 ドル、参加者 15 人までの会が 750 ドル、参加者 20 人までの会が 1,000 ドル、参加者 21 人以上の会が 1,250 ドルとなっています。この情報は正しいですか。至急のご回答をお待ちしております。

敬具

Alton Gilman

送信者：	Myeong Kwan
受信者：	Alton Gilman
日付：	7 月 22 日
件名：	RE: 追ってのご連絡

Gilman 様

土地利用規制に関する研修会をあなたのチームの皆さんに行うことができればうれしいです。私の同僚の Aisha Wright は、当コンサルティング会社で環境への影響に関する研修を担当しており、彼女も対応可能です。私たちは 9 月 27 日と 28 日に協議会に参加する予定です。その 2 日に夜間の研修会を行えるほど協議会の会合が早く終了する保証はありません。ですから、協議会の直前か直後に研修会を設定するのがおそらく一番簡単でしょう。

私は 26 日に研修を行えますし、Wright さんは、私が帰った後も数日アルバータ州に滞在する予定なので、29 日に研修会を行えると思います。E メールに挙げられていた研修料金は正しいです。将来的には、私たちが提供している、環境技術者にとって興味深い他のテーマについての追加のセミナーにもご関心を持たれるかもしれません。例えば、環境的持続可能性の維持やエネルギー効率のよい建造物の建設方法などです。

どの日取りと研修会が御社にとって最適かご確認ください。近いうちにご連絡をお待ちしております。

よろしくお願いします。

Myeong Kwan

研修会予定表	
研修会講師：	Myeong Kwan
日付：	9 月 26 日
時間：	午前 9 時～午後 4 時 30 分 （昼食休憩　午後 0 時～午後 1 時）
場所：	Keats 会議センター 会議室 26B
参加人数：	技術者 18 名

16. 1 通目の E メールの目的は何ですか。

(A) 協議会への出席を確認すること

(B) 研修会の予定を組むことについて問い合わせること

(C) プレゼンテーションを中止すること

(D) ウェブサイトの更新を依頼すること

17. DQR 社について何が示唆されていますか。

(A) 数百人の技術者を雇っている。

(B) 研修に外部のコンサルタントを雇っている。

(C) 国際協議会に資金提供している。

(D) アルバータ州にある。

18. Krestarr グループのアルバータ州での研修料金は幾らになりますか。

(A) 500 ドル

(B) 750 ドル

(C) 1,000 ドル

(D) 1,250 ドル

19. 2 通目の E メールの第 1 段落 3 行目にある "guarantee" に最も意味が近いのは

(A) 許可

(B) 製品保証

(C) 通知

(D) 確約

20. 予定表によると、どの研修会が選択されましたか。

(A) 土地利用規制

(B) 環境への影響

(C) 持続可能性

(D) エネルギー効率のよい建造物

Section

20

123

公式 TOEIC® Listening & Reading トレーニング 2
リーディング編
別冊 正解／訳

2023 年 12 月 6 日　第 1 版第 1 刷発行

著者	ETS
編集協力	株式会社 エディット
	株式会社 群企画
	株式会社 WIT HOUSE
表紙デザイン	山崎 聡
発行元	一般財団法人 国際ビジネスコミュニケーション協会
	〒 100-0014
	東京都千代田区永田町 2-14-2
	山王グランドビル
	電話　(03) 5521-5935
印刷・製本	日経印刷株式会社

ISBN 978-4-906033-73-7